WITHDRAWN

5/12 7x L 4/04   08/17 7x L 7/16

ROYAL OAK PUBLIC LIBRARY
222 EAST ELEVEN MILE ROAD
PO BOX 494
ROYAL OAK, MI 48068-0494
(248) 246-3700

Library Hours
Monday 10-9
Tuesday 10-9
Wednesday 10-9
Thursday 10-9
Friday 10-6
Saturday 10-6

DEMCO

PUBLIC LIBRARY
JUN 0 9 1997
ROYAL OAK, MICH.

DETROIT LIONS
FACTS & TRIVIA™

by
Marc Davis

The E. B. Houchin Company

1996
South Bend, Indiana

The E. B. Houchin Company
23700 Marquette Blvd. A-8
South Bend, Indiana 46628

Copyright 1996 by the Publisher on behalf of the Author

All rights reserved, which include the right
to reproduce this book or any portions thereof
in any form whatsoever without prior written consent
from the publisher.

This book or any information contained herein may not be used
by persons in the electronic media for commercial programming
without prior written consent from the publisher.

ISBN: 0-938313-19-3

First Printing: September 1996

Cover photo by Jim Biever

Collectors cards from Author's private collection

Photos courtesy of the Detroit Lions

Printed in USA

TABLE OF CONTENTS

LIONS HISTORY & TRIVIA	7
Introduction	9
Through the Years	11
1 - Hail the Colors Blue and Silver (1930-34)	13
Trivia Questions	
The Portsmouth Years	19
When the Lions Came to Town	21
The First Season	22
2 - Not Queen, Not Duke, Not Prince (1935-39)	25
Trivia Questions	29
3 - The Lion in Winter (1940-49)	35
Trivia Questions	39
4 - Life in the Fast Layne (1950-57)	45
Trivia Questions - The Golden Age Quiz	56
5 - Mad Duck But No Glory (1958-70)	65
Trivia Questions	70
6 - Look Homeward, Leo (1970-79)	77
Trivia Questions	82
7 - A Sooner in Lions Clothing (1980-83)	89
Trivia Questions	93
8 - The Seven-Year Drought (1984-90)	99
Trivia Questions	101

9 - The House That Wayne Built (1991-Present)	107
Trivia Questions	112
10 - Championship Games	117
Trivia Questions	
December 15, 1935 (versus the New York Giants)	120
December 28, 1952 (at Cleveland)	121
December 27, 1953 (versus Cleveland)	121
December 26, 1954 (at Cleveland)	122
December 29, 1957 (versus Cleveland)	122
11 - The Thanksgiving Day Tradition	123
Trivia Questions	124
Profiles	**127**
1 - Dutch Clark	129
Trivia Questions	130
2 - Bobby Layne	131
Trivia Questions	133
3 - Joe Schmidt	137
Trivia Questions	138
4 - Barry Sanders	141
Trivia Questions	143
GENERAL FACTS & TRIVIA	**147**
1 - The Hall of Fame	149
Trivia Questions	151
2 - Coaches' Corner	155
Coaches' Records	156
Trivia Questions	157
3 - Grab Bag	159

THE RECORD BOOK	**161**
1 - Individual Records	163
Passing	163
Rushing	165
Receiving	167
Kicking	168
Scoring	169
Sacks	170
Interceptions	171
2 - Team Records	172
Season	172
Game - Offense	173
Game - Defense	173
3 - Lions vs. the League	175
Regular Season	175
Post-Season	177
The Answers	**178**
About the Author	**192**

To

Mom and Dad

for buying me my first football helmst
—a Lions helmet—
for Christmas 1978

and to

Jessie

who gets as upset as I do whent he Lions lose

LIONS HISTORY & TRIVIA

BOBBY LAYNE, the epitome of the Detroit Lions.

Introduction

In the beginning, God created the heavens and the earth, and the landscape of pro football was a formless wasteland. The utterance of "Let there be light" began the whole tedious process of inventing the universe as we know it.

Of course, God had a billion or so other issues on the agenda before He could kick around the idea of the first gridiron. But alas, God, in His infinite wisdom, knew a good thing when He came up with it. So the Lord blessed the seventh day, not only for rest and sanctity as the Good Book says, but with a game that consisted of one almost round ball (at the time) and two teams of eleven men created in His image, squaring off, face to face, hand to hand on a grass field.

And the Lord God spoke: "Let there be football."

During the primeval history of the game, God had no inclination to toy with the idea of Astroturf or 100-catch seasons or Jerry Jones for that matter. Of course, pro football expanded and new ideas, new rules were born and old ones died. Leather helmets are gone. Field goals once counted for five points and touchdowns only four. Forward passing used to be illegal. Now the frequency of 3,000-yard passers and 1,000-yard receivers seems to increase every season. Rules have been altered or added to make the game more offense friendly.

My, how the face of the game has changed. Take the Lions for instance. They no longer play in the city of Detroit. They call home a domed stadium where football is played on a carpet instead of the grass of old U-D stadium or Tiger Stadium. The Pontiac Silverdome draws crowds in excess of 70,000 per game in a good year, compared to under 20,000 the year of the Lions' first championship in 1935. You know the times have changed when the Lions offense breaks a slew of long standing team records in one season. Heck, Lions' fans of recent years know the times have changed when the team possesses a formidable passing attack as displayed in 1995 via Scott Mitchell, Herman Moore, Brett Perriman and Company.

Yes, the game has changed. But with change comes the passing of old to new, and that in turn creates history, which creates tradition, which creates legend. The Lions are rich in all of these. There have been many characters and superstars, as much glory as tragedy. There has been frustration. There has been celebration.

Over the years, the Lions have been the good, the bad, the graceful, the ugly. They have legends, stories, and tradition.

The Lord God made them that way.

Through the Years

1
Hail the Colors Blue and Silver (1930-34)

We play our heartstrings like violins and donate our sweat, tears, and nervous systems for the sake of our football team. Sometimes it is best to keep the remote control out of reach and out of firing range of the TV set, especially for fans of the Detroit Lions. For, long after the savoring, and if we're feeling good enough to, after the bragging of victory is gone, the agony of defeat lingers. The plays—all the interceptions or fumbles or missed executions—remain as private little ghosts that haunt our heads throughout the off-season.

So it has seemed for as long as we can remember. But we can exorcize these demons through the recollection of memories. Take me back to the 1950s, and the pains of losing outright or coming close only to be saddened seem to be about as far away as four decades. The Detroit Lions have been a fun team to root for. After all, nobody else has Barry Sanders. Nobody else had Alex Karras or Joe Schmidt. And nobody else had Bobby Layne during their glory days. These are only some of the players who decorate Lions heritage with greatness, the men who have provided some of the team's defining moments; defining moments that have made all the struggles and pain worth the efforts. Yes, there is redemption in loyalty.

One of the team's earliest defining moments came on Thanksgiving day of the Lions' first year in town. The game on October 29, 1934 versus the defending league champion Chicago Bears was a promising showcase of the team to its new city. At 10-1, the Lions had proved that they were a winning club. If they could beat the Bears, who entered the game in first place at 11-0, the Lions' hopes of bringing home a championship would ignite the town's interest. If they lost, title hopes would be smothered. Stoking the fire a little, Potsy Clark, head coach of the Lions, had declared two weeks before the game that the Lions would feast on "Bear meat" for Thanksgiving. A lot was at stake for the Lions, and the outcome came down to one play.

Late in the fourth quarter, the Bears took a 19-16 lead. But the Lions were undaunted by the change of momentum. With the ball lodged on their own 20 yard line, the Lions began to smash through the Bears' defense. Thanks to the precision running and passing of Ace Gutowsky and Dutch Clark, the Lions chalked up five first downs, until they penetrated to the Bears' 14. Inside the last minute of the game, the situation called for a game-tying field goal. Perhaps mindful of his boast two weeks earlier, Potsy made a gutsy decision to go for the touchdown, the victory, and the "Bear meat" all in one final, desperate play.

The football team fielded that day was not born in Detroit. The Lions were once the Spartans. The Spartans' hometown of Portsmouth, Ohio, located a couple hundred miles south of Detroit, had a small time atmosphere where supporting a professional football team made about as much sense as taking a boat with a hole in it out into the harbor. For a few years up to 1929, Portsmouth played as an independent pro team. Former player-coach of that independent team, Hal Griffen became one of the team's owners, as well as coach, when the Spartans entered the NFL in 1930. Back then, the offensive philosophy was to run the ball at your opponent until their noses bled. The Spartans had a strong backfield but little else. Under Griffen, they finished eighth out of eleven teams at 5-6-3.

Their second year in the NFL brought a considerable leap in talent and progress. Potsy Clark took over as head coach. The biggest addition was Dutch Clark, who had been a star tailback at Colorado College. His cat-quick reflexes enabled him to elude the best of tacklers. Not on par with, say, Barry Sanders, but then, no one ever could be. Dutch was, however, one of the best runners of his time. With him as the Spartans' main weapon, the small town team was ready to contend. But their 11-3 record fell short as they finished behind the 12-2 Green Bay Packers.

Potsy Clark stressed conditioning, and he cracked the whip accordingly during workouts. It paid off. While the Spartan teams were not loaded with "big guns" like the elite teams in the NFL, their confidence and stamina was unrivaled.

Portsmouth won six games the following year, with only one defeat and four ties. A key victory during the season came against the Packers on December 4, in which the Spartans earned their nickname, the "Iron Men". During the game, Potsy Clark refused to make substitutions. From start to finish, the same 11 Spartans remained on the battlefield, disrupting and frustrating their opponents along the way. The Packer offense completed one pass in 16 attempts. The 9-0 victory gave Portsmouth a tie for the title with the Chicago Bears.

That was an intriguing year, for the Spartans and Bears participated in the first playoff game in NFL history. Unfortunately, the post-season game came at a bad time for Potsy Clark's team. Due to a previous agreement to coach basketball at Colorado College, star Dutch Clark was unable to play in the game. Their offense was flat without its sparkplug, and the Spartan machine failed to score: Bears 9, Lions 0. Since the game counted in the season standings for 1932, both Chicago and Green Bay had a better winning percentage than Portsmouth. The Spartans wound up in third place.

During the game, on the Bears' touchdown, Bronko Nagurski threw what Portsmouth thought was an illegal pass. NFL rules at the time stipulated that a pass must be attempted from five or more yards behind the line of scrimmage. To no avail, Potsy Clark argued that Nagurski had stepped well beyond the allowed yardage. The play's significance would be felt one year later when the five-yard rule was dropped. Passes could now be attempted from anywhere behind the line of scrimmage. Why not? As Potsy Clark had stated during the annual league meetings in the off-season: "Nagurski will pass from anywhere, so we might as well make it legal." The idea of a post-season game to determine the NFL champion stuck around as well after 1932.

The 1933 season brought the dividing of the NFL. Instead of 10 teams bunched together in the standings, there were now two divisions made up of five teams each: the East and West. The Spartans ended up in the West division, along with double nemesis Green Bay and Chicago. Before the first game, news surfaced that Dutch Clark had quit football to stay on as athletic director at the Colorado School of Mines. Veteran Glenn Presnell took over Clark's role, leading the team to a second place finish. This time the Spartans trailed only the league champion Chicago Bears in the standings. The 6-5 record was the team's last hurrah in Portsmouth as financial troubles set in.

Financial doom had lingered from the outset. Paychecks were often hard to come by for players. Area businessmen who owned stock in the club would throw in cash to try and keep the franchise afloat, but it did not help matters that only a couple thousand fans, a mere one-fourth of the stadium's capacity, would pay to see the actual games. But who could blame them when scrimmages could be watched for free on Fridays? In the end, the club was nearly bankrupt.

Three men would be instrumental in moving the sinking team to Detroit. The first phase began during a meeting between the vice president and general manager of the Columbus baseball franchise, Joe Carr, who, during the financially tough times of the Depression, held down a second job as president of the NFL, and H.G. Salsinger, sports editor of the *Detroit News*. Carr, concerned about increasing professional football's popularity, had viewed Detroit as a top sports town, since hockey's Red Wings and baseball's Tigers were prominent fixtures with the people of the city. So he told Salsinger about the troubles of the team in Portsmouth. Salsinger was determined to help the NFL find a new location for the Spartans. He acted quickly by setting up a committee in Detroit, comprised of other journalists and some of the major sportsmen of the area. As history, or fate if you like, would have it, the committee saw Leo J. Fitzpatrick at the Detroit Athletic Club. The importance of Fitzpatrick's role was basically as a set up man. His boss was George A. "Dick" Richards, owner of WJR radio station. Richards was a known football fan and, more importantly for the committee, had become a wealthy man by starting an auto dealership in town, then, after making a success of the company, selling it to General Motors for the hefty price tag of $100,000. Fitzpatrick ran the idea by the radio mogul, and Salsinger's search for an interested party with enough financial backing to buy an impoverished franchise had ended.

In order to purchase the club, Richards spearheaded a syndicate that included over 20 of the top businessmen of the area, big names with a lot of clout. Among them were the president of Pontiac Motor Co., Harry Klinger, and L.P. Fischer, president of the Cadillac Motor Company. Joe Carr officially awarded Richards the old Portsmouth team at the league meetings in New York on June 30, 1934. Richards, his syndicate, and the city of Detroit had a new football team that, by all standards, was an accomplished pro club.

There was never much of a doubt in the minds of these men, particularly Carr, Salsinger, and Richards, that the pro game would become popular in the area. Just how long would it take?

The signs of the times were shut down businesses, low wages, people selling food or peddling junk on sidewalks. 1934 found the Depression breaking the nation's back as Americans worked hard to get a hold of a better tomorrow. Would the people pay hard earned money to watch a local pro team play a game that still trailed the collegiate version in both popularity and respect? Sure, it was an opportunity to enlighten fans on the attractiveness of the pro circuit, but would timing be a hindrance once more? After all, pro football had died in Detroit on three occasions before the Lions.

The first attempt at fielding a pro eleven that carried the city's name was as unceremonious as a group of boys gathering in a school yard for a pickup game. It came at the inopportune time of professional football's earliest try at organizing a league. The name of the league was the American Professional Football Association. Two years later, it would be renamed the NFL. The condition of the sport was the main crutch for the Detroit Heralds, who were considered "unofficials" of the APFA in 1920. They were recognized as part of the 1920 season since they played enough games against league members. That year, there were 10 charter members of the APFA, including the oldest franchises in the NFL, the Chicago Cardinals (now playing in Arizona) and the Chicago Bears. Each team paid a $100 entry fee. Like the Heralds, three other teams had an "unofficial" status in the league: the Buffalo All-Americans, Columbus Panhandles, and Chicago Tigers.

There was not much interest in professional football in Detroit during the early '20s. Most people were trying to piece their lives back together after World War I. Home crowds diminished from week to week until support all but disappeared. The Heralds finished out two seasons with a 2-8-1 record.

For $500, Jimmy Conzelman was awarded a Detroit franchise on August 1, 1925. Using some of the best talent in town, the Detroit Panthers were a success on the field. The NFL had grown to 20 teams that year, and Conzelman's Panthers posted an impressive 8-2-2 record versus the league, good for third place. Bad weather washed away any plans of a financial victory as the Panthers were rained on for seven consecutive home games.

Another attempt was made in 1926, minus gray skies. By then, the new look team fielded by Conzelman was as washed up as the field was the previous year. A 4-6-2 record was the result. Conzelman, who would go on to win a championship with the Providence Steamrollers in 1928, later admitted that Detroit simply was not ready for the pro game at that time. The team folded on July 27, 1927.

Next came Benny Friedman's try at settling into the area's sports niche. Friedman's application for reinstatement for a Detroit franchise was approved on August 12, 1928. Deriving from the fame of his college football days at Michigan, he named his city sponsored team the Wolverines. Most of the players collected for the franchise were area stars whose best days were behind them. The Detroit Wolverines eventually became a road team only. At 7-2-1, they ended their existence as a third place team with little fan support.

So the failures of his predecessors paved the way for Richards in 1934. This was it. How could a ready made team that challenged for a title two years before fail in a great sports town anyway? A big plus for the team was the return of Dutch Clark, who came out of a one year retirement to play for Richards.

The Lions were drawing 12,000 fans or fewer for home games their first year, despite their flawless play. It was not until the Thanksgiving game that the people of Detroit saw they had a team they could roar about, one that could become as beloved as the Tigers were. A sold out University of Detroit Stadium, 26,000 strong, some of them cheering along the boundary lines of the end zones, witnessed their home team pull out to a surprising 16-7 half-time lead over the league champion Bears. Two touchdowns by fullback Ace Gutowsky gave Detroit visions of an upset. He ran for 85 yards in the game and intercepted a pass. It was the biggest half-time deficit for Chicago in three years. A test of the Lions' character came on their final drive after falling behind 19-16. Inside Chicago's 15, Potsy Clark could smell "Bear meat." Electing to go for the win outright, the Lions' final play of the game was a Glenn Presnell pass into the end zone. As the ball fell incomplete, the Lions' hopes for a title were dashed.

They played like champions that day. A win would have increased football fever throughout town a bit more rapidly perhaps, but the performance of the home team in that one game alone won the fan's hearts. It was the first sign that professional football was going to be a success in Detroit

In the rematch three days later in Chicago, the Bears pulled out another close game, 10-7. Detroit finished 10-3 for the season, good for second place. But it was a sign of things to come. The Lions proved they could play with the best the league had to offer. They were on the brink of glory, and hungry to achieve it.

The Lions' first Thanksgiving game serves as a good introduction into the history of the franchise. As there has been throughout the decades of the Lions' existence, there was greatness in that game. There was tradition and heartbreak as well.

TRIVIA QUESTIONS

THE PORTSMOUTH YEARS
1. What main color did the Spartans wear?

2. What was Potsy Clark's first name?

3. Potsy coached for what Indianapolis university prior to his stint with Portsmouth?

4. Who played quarterback for the inaugural Spartan team and later played defensive back for the Lions in '34?

5. What were his two nicknames?

6. Where did he play college ball?

7. When the Spartans joined the NFL in 1930, they kept one arch rival independent team on their schedule. The two teams met three times for exhibition games during the regular season, with Portsmouth winning twice. What team was this?

8. On July 11, 1931, the NFL fined the Spartans, Packers, and Bears for breaking what league policy?

9. How much was the fine for each club?

10. The first official All-NFL team came out in 1931. The honorees were selected in the ninth annual *Green Bay Press-Gazette* Poll. Among those making the choices were coaches, team and game officials, and sportswriters. What two Spartans were named to the team?

11. The Spartans won 11 games in 1931, while Green Bay won 12. On the Spartans 1932 yearbook, they claimed themselves to be co-champions of the NFL. Why was this?

12. What center did the Spartans pick up from the Chicago Cardinals in 1932?

13. Where was the historic 1932 playoff game between the Bears and Spartans held?

14. Why was the game played there?

15. Although he missed the final post-season game, Dutch Clark led the NFL in scoring in 1932. How many points did he score?

WHEN THE LIONS CAME TO TOWN

1. That fateful meeting between NFL president Joe Carr and *Detroit News* sports editor H.G. Salsinger took place at what yearly function?

2. How much was the franchise fee to transfer the team to Detroit?

3. How many players did Richards take title to when he purchased the Spartans?

4. In what way did Richards decide to come up with a new name for the Spartans?

5. Why was "Lions" chosen as a suitable moniker?

6. Who became the Lions vice-president and general manager after the move from Portsmouth?

7. After the syndicate took over as owners of the new Detroit team, William F. Fox, Jr., writing in the *Indianapolis News,* joked that after a few board meetings, coach Potsy Clark would have a hard time figuring out a certain kind of something to own. What was the item Fox was referring to?

8. The Lions contracted to play their home games at the University of Detroit Stadium. What was the capacity of the stadium?

9. How many years did the original lease run?

10. What was the general admission cost of tickets to home games?

11. How much did programs cost?

12. The Lions played in the NFL's Western Division in 1934. What other four teams made up the division that year?

13. The Detroit Zoo donated two lion cubs as mascots. What were their names?

14. Thanks to public relations man Tommy Emmett and John Millen of the Detroit Zoo, who was given a football and a jersey, and, according to Jack Weeks of the *Detroit Free Press*, was signed "to play roving center on defense and handle the forward passing attack?"

15. Who were the four original Lions cheerleaders?

16. Richards wanted the cheerleaders to wear lion costumes, but the cost of $300 apiece was too steep for him. So Richards purchased only one suit. Which of the cheerleaders did he choose to wear the costume, and what was his criteria in deciding?

17. How many players reported to the Lions' first training camp?

18. Before the first season game, the roster had to be trimmed to the NFL limit. What was the limit Potsy Clark had to get down to?

19. What was the title of Potsy Clark's column in the *Detroit News*?

20. What other role did Potsy serve for the team?

21. Who was the Lions public address announcer?

THE FIRST SEASON
1. Before the start of their first NFL season, the Lions played an exhibition in a northern Michigan town. Who were the Lions' opponents?

2. What famous orchestra leader canceled a New York radio show in order to be at the home opener?

3. Who did Detroit play in their season opener?

4. What was the score of the game, and who scored the Lions' points?

5. In the third week of the season, Detroit traveled to Green Bay and beat the Packers, 3-0. Who kicked the game winning field goal and how long was it?

6. How many games in a row did the Lions win at the start of the season?

7. How many consecutive games did they win by shutout to start the year?

8. What team finally broke the scoreless string?

9. How many yards did the Lions rush for that day during a 40-7 triumph?

10. One of the Lions home games was not played in Detroit. Where was the game played?

11. In that game, how many yards did Dutch Clark rush for?

12. On November 18, the Lions beat the Cincinnati-St. Louis Reds, 40-7, at U-D Stadium. What organization did the Lions donate the profits of the game to?

13. How many games were played in Detroit the first season?

14. Visiting clubs received how much money from the Lions in order for the teams to come play in Detroit?

15. Per game, what was the team payroll?

16. How many TD passes did the Lions throw all year?

17. Who were the Lions who made all-pro in 1934?

18. What was Ace Gutowsky's first name?

19. What country was Ace born in?

20. What was Grover Emerson's nickname?

21. What was George Christensen's nickname?

22. What was John Schneller's nickname?

What college or university did each play for?

23. Glenn Presnell

24. George Christensen

25. Ernie Caddel

26. Potsy Clark

Name the uniform numbers of each:

27. Glenn Presnell

28. Ace Gutowsky

29. Ernie Caddel

30. Jo Mendi

2
Not Queen, Not Duke, Not Prince (1935-39)

It's a good thing natural selection chose the lion as king of beasts, since such a reputation made the use of its name for a football team inevitable. For some reason, the Detroit Elephants just doesn't sound right.

Bert Lahr's performance in *The Wizard of Oz* aside, the lion has long been used as a symbol of power, nobility, admiration. After all, you wouldn't find any lions at the bottom of the food chain; just ask a poor, overwhelmed warthog about that (re: *The Lion King*). Metro-Goldwyn-Mayer—better known by its acronym, MGM—the legendary motion picture company that had "more stars than there are in heaven," used a roaring lion named Leo as a trademark to open every one of its glorious films. Egyptian sphinxes have the heads of ancient rulers and a lion's body that represents the pharaoh's strength. In fact, Pharaoh Ramses II, who reigned from 1290-1224 B.C., took a lion into battle as his army's mascot. Aslan, the lord and savior of C. S. Lewis's fabled Narnia was a lion. More examples could be made, but the list would reach the end of this chapter.

It was apparent early on that the Detroit franchise had been aptly named. The team roamed the football jungle of the 1930s with courage as well as talent and ferocity. It was an ensemble for the ages: Dutch Clark, the leader; a tough defense; a bullish running attack; and Potsy Clark, the brains of the whole outfit.

With their rookie season in Detroit a success, both competitively and with the town's population, the Lions set their sights on NFL immortality. After two tight losses to the Chicago Bears ended their season as Western Division bridesmaids, G.A. Richards invited the fans to bet money on the Lions beating the Bears in '35. He even guaranteed it by promising to pay off the debts if his team failed.

Of course, Richards had a plan. At least, he had a scheme. It was evident to Richards that the main hurdle for the Lions was Chicago's Bronko Nagurski. The Bears fullback had thrown one TD and scored another in the two Chicago victories. As the story goes, Richards arranged to have drinks with Nagurski and George Halas, coach of the Bears, in New York shortly after the season ended. He proceeded to offer Nagurski a $10,000 payoff to quit the sport for the upcoming season. Well, Bronko easily turned down the bribe, but Richards made it clear that he was willing to play hard ball and had no qualms about pitching high and inside once in awhile. Halas and Richards were fast becoming enemies. It was a rift that would boil over and come to a head four years later.

The stage was set for November 24, with the Lions traveling to Chicago owning a 5-3-1 record. The Bears entered the game at 5-3. Destiny has a peculiar way of throwing its hand into the mix. Or maybe destiny just loves irony. Bronko Nagurski ended up missing a majority of the season with a hip injury. George Richards's obstacle had been removed due to the sheer nature of the game. And he still had a fat wallet.

The Lions fought Chicago to a 20-20 tie. Coming off a split with Green Bay the previous two games, the tie kept Detroit in contention. The Bears and Lions swapped home fields for the rematch. Like the year before, it was a Thanksgiving Day special. It turned out to be the Lions' first Turkey Day victory and first win over the Bears. The 14-2 score made George Richards a man of his words. Riding on the virtues of that big win, the following week the Lions stampeded the Brooklyn Dodgers, 28-0, to move ahead of the Chicago Cardinals and Green Bay Packers for the division title.

The Lions of '35 overpowered their opponents with a viable ground game. Four of the NFL's top ten rushers were members of the blue-and-silver. George Halas called the Lions' attack, "the best offense in the game." It has often been said, even nowadays, that the way to a championship is on the ground. The Lions bullied and battered their way to the top with their stable of thoroughbred racers and line-bucking blockers. No match for the Lions' power and speed game, the New York Giants bowed out, 26-7, in the Championship final on December 15, 1935.

Looking back on the first two seasons of Lions' football, Dutch Clark made this observation: "I think we had a better team in 1934 than we did in 1935."

It may have been an all-around better team, but in 1935, the Detroit Lions were champions of the NFL.

They continued to be contenders for the next three seasons. The main chink in their armor could be attributed to inner turmoil. Sure, some of the finger-pointing could be leveled at the injuries the team sustained. Late season games in 1936 were played without the services of Ace Gutowsky, Ernie Caddel, and center/linebacker Clare Randolph. But the major problems cascaded from the top down. Evidence that the franchise had soured a little after the championship came when, after a third place finish in the '36 season, Potsy Clark resigned. He switched cities by becoming coach of the Brooklyn Dodgers. Potsy's departure left a bad taste in Richards's mouth. Perhaps out of spite more than anything, as was now becoming customary for the brash owner, G. A. Richards declared victory over Potsy's Dodgers prior to the start of the next season.

Clark had endured a love-hate, tug-of-war relationship with the volatile Detroit owner during his three-year stint as head coach. It had been rumored that Potsy had either quit or had been fired numerous times during his stay, only to have things ironed out in time to save the relationship. Brooklyn, at least, was far enough away for peace of mind.

So, if one Clark skips town, you replace him with another one. Richards quickly promoted legendary Dutch Clark to the post of player-coach. It was a tailor-made fit; that is, until Dutch received a dose of Richards's infamous treatment.

If you think Jerry Jones has a fetish for meddling with the game day operations, I'd like to introduce you to Mr. George Richards, his predecessor by almost 60 years. At the time Dutch took over as head coach, Richards's poor health forced him to stay at home. It did not stop him from getting messages to coach Clark by using his chauffeur as a delivery boy. The notes often criticized the coach for his play calling and almost always second guessed his moves. The offense was boring and obvious, he would say. Then, Richards would write his own solutions as to how the team should be run. Eventually, the owner's slipping health prompted him to move to Los Angeles. Long distance phone calls were made to Dutch on a regular basis. In order to stay abreast of all that the team was doing, Richards hired Harry Wismer to watch over the Lions and give him daily reports. If he heard about something he did not like, Richards would phone Clark immediately and demand explanations. Dutch later revealed Richards's desire to bet on Lions' games and to convince some of the players to go in on the bets, believing the team would play harder for the sake of extra cash. Another famous story about Richards was the time he had a loud speaker rigged up in the locker room before a big game, so he could "inspire" his players with a pep talk.

Can you say control freak?

Multiple distractions are enough to interfere with the good of any team, and Richards constant interruptions marred the remainder of Dutch Clark's stay. Sure, Detroit challenged in '37 and '38 with the old standbys, but the machine was quickly being dismantled. In 1937, the Lions won seven of 11 games and tied for second with the Packers in the Western Division. 1938 saw a repeat performance at 7-4, good for second place. Most significant that year was the decision to move out of U-D Stadium for the more spacious confines of Briggs Stadium. It was like moving out of a one room apartment and into a duplex, considering that the stadium housed two teams: the Lions and the Tigers. Of course, the games were drawing bigger crowds now. That's what the arrival of better economic times can do for a franchise. Winning a championship and fielding star players doesn't hurt either. The fans were ready for more of the winning tradition they had all ready tasted. Too bad the team was locked in turmoil.

Dutch Clark had his supporters as well as some detractors. Alex Wojciechowicz was one player who was not impressed with Clark's coaching philosophies. He later recounted those days by admitting that Dutch did not teach much of the trade to his rookies, that the former running star was so gung-ho on smashing the ball through the defense that the Lions suffered from a one-dimensional attack. Others believed he was a purist. At the time, the players did not want their feelings to interfere with the progress of the team. There were not about to be any mutinies.

Still, by the end of the 1938 season, as Potsy had two years before, Dutch had become fed up. Rumors persisted of Richards's plan to fire him. Before that could happen, Dutch resigned to accept an offer as head coach of the Cleveland Rams. Remaining stars were aging or began to depart from the team as well.

Gus Henderson was appointed as the new head coach of the Detroit Lions for the 1939 season. He inherited a skeleton of the former team that had been one of the best in the game. Many people were critical of Richards's choice, stemming mostly from Henderson's lack of experience on the professional level. He came to town with a resume as a college and minor league pro coach. His leadership qualities proved to be adequate in taking the slipping Lions to a 6-5 record, but it was a far cry from the title-contending team the fans had come to expect. After a fast 6-1 start, the season had bottomed out during the last half of the schedule, with a four-game skid that turned the year into a disaster. It was a foreshadowing of things to come in the next decade.

At least, for one year in their first decade in Detroit, the Lions were second to no one. They were nothing less than kings of the football world.

TRIVIA QUESTIONS

1935-39

1. The 1935 season opener was played against Philadelphia, in which the Lions blanked the Eagles, 35-0. How many first downs did the Lions' defense allow in the game?

2. How many rushing yards did the Lions hold the Brooklyn Dodgers to in a 28-0 victory on December 1, 1935?

3. What offensive feat did the Lions achieve throughout that year's schedule that no other team in the NFL could duplicate?

4. How many interceptions did the Lions register as a team that year?

5. Who led the team in scoring TDs in '35?

6. Who led the team in passing that year with 417 yards?

7. He played for another team prior to the season. What team did he play for?

8. Who led the team in rushing and receiving yards in 1935?

9. What four Lions' runners were in the top 10 of NFL rushers that year?

10. How many shutouts did the team register in 1935?

11. Who led the team in extra point conversions during that season with 16?

12. The Lions traveled 12,000 miles to play exhibition games after winning the 1935 Championship game. How many games did they play on the trip?

13. In a charity benefit game, the Lions championship team played against the College All-Stars team in early '36. What was the result of that game?

14. What was James Stacy's nickname?

15. On November 15, 1936, in a home game against the New York Giants, what team record did Bill Shepherd set?

16. What two Lions made the All-League team in 1936?

17. The Lions set a team record for rushing that season. How many yards did the Lions' runners total?

18. The Lions also set a franchise mark that year for most consecutive road games, which remains intact today. What is that record, and where did the road trip begin?

19. What was the Lions' record during that stretch of away games?

20. The Lions led the NFL in seven offensive categories in 1936. Name four of the seven categories.

21. That same year, Ace Gutowsky set a then team record for most rushing yards by a player in one season. What was his total?

22. How long did the record stand?

23. Dutch Clark led the team with 467 yards passing on 38 completions. How many of those completions were for scores?

24. How many of his passes were interceptions?

25. The NFL draft of collegiate players began in 1936. Who was the Lions' first ever draft pick?

26. After appointing Dutch head coach, George Richards hired a personal publicity man for Clark. Who was he?

27. On October 10, 1937, the Lions defeated the Pittsburgh Pirates, 7-3, at home. How many passing yards did the defense allow?

28. After Dutch became head coach, G. A. Richards declared: "I'll pick Dutch Clark's Lions to beat Potsy Clark's Dodgers every time they meet." The two teams met only once, October 17, 1937, while

Dutch was head coach. What was the outcome of the game?

29. One of the Lions' touchdowns was a 100-yard interception return. Name the Lions' defensive back who scored the TD.

30. The Lions lost four games that year. What teams did they lose to?

31. Who threw the most TDs for the Lions that year?

32. As a team, how many touchdown passes did the Lions throw in 1937?

33. Again the Lions led the league in rushing TDs. How many did they have for the 1937 season?

34. Who was the team's number one pick after the season?

35. What sports editor of the *Detroit Times* quit his job with the paper to become vice president of the Lions on July 3, 1938?

36. How much did unreserved seats sell for during the first season at Briggs Stadium?

37. The first game played at Briggs Stadium was on October 18, 1938 against the Washington Redskins. Which team won the game, and what was the score?

38. Who led the Lions in scoring for the '38 season?

39. Alex Wojciechowicz joined the Lions after the '38 draft. What two positions did he thrive at?

40. The rocky relationship between Richards and Dutch Clark reached a boiling point when they disagreed over trying to acquire an available player from another team. Richards wanted him, insisting the team needed an offensive boost. Clark felt the offense was good

enough as it was. Clark won the argument eventually, and the player was not acquired at that time. Who was this player?

41. What was Gus Henderson's first name?

42. What was his nickname?

43. What Lions' running back called it quits prior to the 1939 season?

44. George Christensen, who had played four seasons in Detroit at tackle, left the Lions before the '39 season to become an assistant coach with what team?

45. How did Ace Gutowsky depart from the team? What team did he go to?

46. Bill Shepherd became the first Lions' player to lead the team in rushing for two straight seasons. What were his rushing yardage totals for each of the two seasons?

47. With Dutch Clark gone, who led the team in scoring for the 1939 season?

48. Who led the Lions in passing yardage and rushing TDs that year?

49. What Lions' record did he set during the season?

50. What incident led to Gus Henderson's firing after the '39 season?

51. What player did Richards covet in the 1939 NFL draft?

52. What college did this player attend, and what position did he play?

53. What price did the Lions' organization pay for this incident?

54. Who did the Lions draft in the first round?

55. How many seasons did he play for Detroit?

What college or University did each play for?

56. Buddy Parker

57. Butch Morse

58. Dwight Sloan

59. Vern Huffman

60. Bill Shepherd

3
The Lion in Winter
(1940-49)

It rained hard in the autumn of 1940 for the Detroit Lions. The concrete foundation of a team that had won early, including a championship in 1935, and had been home to some of football's brightest stars, had turned to mud. The Lions' slide from prominence began the year before, with a season-ending collapse on the field and a battle with the league off the field. 1940 was the team's first losing season.

Winter came to Detroit in the form of their professional football team going into a decade-long hibernation, with a mediocre thawing once or twice, a mere awakening of a restless animal to sustain a yawn of seasons past. It was a decade of bad luck, bad breaks, poor gambles, and unequivocally poor teams. There were some players who would step in to raise memorable masts in the frozen ocean, but for the most part, the Lions could have rolled over and played dead. A little harsh maybe, but this was a team that would have a losing record for seven of 10 seasons throughout the '40s.

The first memorable player was Byron "Whizzer" White.

Before the "Whizzer" became a Lion, the team had gone through its first major organizational transition. Still smarting from the fine slapped on his club for tampering with Bulldog Turner, and with his health worsening, George Richards sold the Lions on February 10, 1940, for a profit of $200,000 more than he had originally purchased the Spartans for six years earlier. Ironically, the sale had to wait for approval by the league until Richards paid off his fine for the Turner fiasco. So the grudge with Halas ultimately had played a significant part in Richards' football demise. Then again, the owner's popularity in NFL circles was so sparse by that time that other enemies would have happily contributed to the cause. Sure, it's easy to shoot bullets through his reputation, but Detroit sports fans are indebted to Richards for taking the bold steps that have led to the town being furnished with a memorable football team.

The new owner was Fred Mandel, a proprietor of a department store in Chicago. The revolving door process by which he tried out coaches showed that Mandel was a tinkerer of grand proportions. Unfortunately, the transformation of the team under the new ownership would be comparable to a plastic surgeon giving a bad face-lift to a struggling movie star. And the guy was no tightwad, either. In fact, Mandel, who frequently tried to buy a better team, would end up losing a good deal of money on the franchise by the time it came for him to sell.

In an effort to bring back the glory of the early days, Mandel's first action was to re-hire Potsy Clark as head coach. With the biggest piece of the puzzle intact, the organization then paid the Pittsburgh Pirates (soon to be renamed the Steelers) for the playing rights of White. The "Whizzer" turned out to be a gem, leading the NFL in rushing in 1940—the first Lion to do so—with 514 yards. He scored five touchdowns and played brilliantly on defense and punt returns. Perhaps the greatest asset he brought to the team was a die-hard spirit that allowed him to play with injuries that would have confined most mortal men to crutches. He was a quick-witted, imaginative athlete who was worth every dollar spent on him. Two seasons worth of dollars, actually. Again, he led the Lions in rushing the next year, but was out of professional football altogether before the '42 season, soon to pursue a law career that would land him a seat on the U.S. Supreme Court.

Despite Whizzer's magic, the Lions could only muster a respectable 5-5-1 season in 1940. Potsy resigned, and the team was left looking for a new direction.

News that would forever change life in America reached the States on December 7, 1941. Japan had bombed Pearl Harbor at about 7:55 a.m. (Hawaii time), sending America headlong into World War II. Pro football would also feel the loss suffered from the conflict, as players began swapping jerseys for fatigues.

But the National Football League did march on, even if the talent had been scaled down. At least it offered the nation some kind of distraction from the war once or twice a week.

The Lions trudged on as well. Bill Edwards was given control of the team after Potsy left and promptly steered Detroit to its first ever losing season. At best, 1941 was an up-and-down year, one full of hard-fought victories and crushing defeats. The Lions could not handle the likes of Green Bay and the Chicago Bears, scoring a paltry 14 points in the four meetings with them and allowing a combined 120.

If the 4-6-1 record that year indicated that Edwards had guided the team a little further off course, then 1942 was a football disaster tantamount to the sinking of the *Titanic*. At 0-11, you can't go any lower than rock bottom. Edwards, who suffered from a lack of talent, most of which vanished during the off-season to aid the war effort, was replaced during the sorry campaign by assistant coach John Karcis. The divine spirits above were in no mood for miracles that season, as the offensive numbers would indicate. The scoring totals for the year: five touchdowns, one field goal.

With the Lions' winter slumber reaching its third season, Mandel tried desperately to breath life into his team. By hiring Gus Dorais to replace Karcis, Mandel had achieved something Richards was unable to do. Five years before in 1938, the head coach of the University of Detroit rejected Richards's proposal to coach the Lions. Now, he inherited a much worse team, but had the job security of a long-term deal needed to build a winner.

His first year brought a 3-6-1 improvement. By the start of the season, Detroit had been able to field a better team than the depleted '42 version. Along with all-pro center and linebacker Alex Wojciechowicz and veteran running back Lloyd Cardwell, the Lions now featured 1942 Heisman trophy winner Frank Sinkwich.

In 1944, Detroit created some momentum in the final games of the season behind the Sinkwich-led offense. A 5-0 spurt at the end gave the Lions a 6-3-1 record, a second place tie with the Bears, and fans had a premature indication that spring had arrived. In a war-weakened season, Sinkwich threw 12 touchdowns, scored six others, and booted 24 extra points and two field goals on his way to winning the league's Most Valuable Player award. He was also the leading punter and near the top for punt returning.

After one failed attempt the year before, Frank Sinkwich was accepted by the Army in 1945. The Lions lost him for good after the war ended when he switched over to the newly formed All-America Football Conference to play for the New York Yankees. Still, Dorais managed to find the right formula, using standouts such as Charles Fenenbock at tailback and Bob Westfall at fullback, both of whom reaped the benefits of a powerful line. Despite a porous secondary that was eaten alive all season, the result was the Lions' best showing since its championship season. At 7-3, the Lions finished behind the eventual National Football League champion Cleveland Rams in the Western Division.

With football's soldiers returning from the battlefields of real war in '46, the Lions crawled comfortably back into their den for a prolonged winter's nap. Actually, the culprit was a string of pre-season injuries to top players. Detroit tumbled to a 1-10 mark, and dusted out the cellar for a three-year stay.

Mandel reached deep into his pockets once more to try and reverse the team's fortunes. Again, he struck a deal with the Pittsburgh Steelers, this time in an effort to obtain the rights to talk to star tailback Bill Dudley. Dudley had announced his retirement from playing to coach at Virginia, his alma mater. Mandel made him an offer he couldn't refuse, and Dudley had a fair year in 1947 with the blue-and-silver. Nothing Dudley, or any of the players could do, prevented the team from claiming another washout season. The Lions won only three games all year, while coming up short nine times.

Over the years, it had become increasingly apparent to Mandel that making money on the franchise was a lost cause. On December 17, 1947, Gus Dorais was asked to resign, but he refused to step down. The language of a contract extension he had worked out a year before entitled him to full payment of the remaining years if he was fired. It added up to $25,000 for the four years left on the agreement. After weeks of disputing back and forth, Mandel had no choice but to pay the settlement.

It was time to bail out of the money eating franchise. Mandel sold the Lions to a group of Detroit businessmen. Since Detroit is known as the "Motor City," it was only fitting that once again the syndicate included several investors from the automobile industry. The new ownership was headed by D. Lyle Fife and Edwin J. Anderson. Fife ran an electrical products company, and Anderson was the president of the Goebel Brewing Company. Originally, Fife held the position of club president, while Anderson resided as vice-president. One year later, Fife would be replaced by Anderson. This set off a power struggle that would last midway through the next decade.

The first objective for the new owners was reached when the Lions named Bo McMillan the architect for rebuilding the toothless franchise. His presence would not be felt until the following year, as the autumn of '48 turned into an abysmal 2-10 campaign.

An improvement to 4-8 and a step up to fourth place followed, but did not result in much of a cash flow for the organization. By now fans were hungry, but the hapless play of the team kept the majority of them away.

McMillan's tenure was plagued by a number of problems, most noticeably his own frustrations at relating to the players and handling the dominant presence of the ownership. Most players demonstrated an open resentment toward the strict atmosphere at Camp McMillan, and his failure to display a likable personality would be his undoing. But one thing McMillan had going for him was an uncanny foresight that would produce many of the legends of the '50s.

It was in April of 1950 that Bobby Layne came to town, the harbinger of a glorious new morning—one with green pastures, and a fresh scent of spring in the industrial air over Detroit.

TRIVIA QUESTIONS

1940-49

1. Who did Fred Mandel appoint president of the club?

2. Before the Lions traded for the rights to Whizzer White, he had been overseas studying at an esteemed university as a Rhodes scholar. What university was this?

3. How much did Mandel pay Pittsburgh for the rights to Whizzer White?

4. What was the Whizzer's famed trick play on punt returns?

5. What honor was White decorated with for his service in WWII?

6. Who was the only Lion who did not register for the draft in 1940? This includes all players, coaches, and members of the front office.

7. In the first game of the 1940 season, the Lions played to a 0-0 tie with the Chicago Cardinals. How many yards did the Lions' defense allow that day?

8. What was the Lions' main handicap in the game?

9. Who led the team in passing yards for the 1940 season?

10. Why did Potsy Clark resign again at the end of the season?

11. What university did Bill Edwards coach at before coming to the Lions?

12. On November 23, 1941, in a game against the Bears, what Lions' record did Bill Jefferson set?

13. November 29, 1941 was Whizzer White's final game. The Lions' opponents that day were the Chicago Cardinals. How did White score his touchdown during the game? How long was his touchdown pass in the third quarter and who caught it? What was the final score of the game?

14. How old was White when he quit football?

15. Name three of the five Lions' players who were ordered to report for military service at the end of the '41 season.

16. Two Lions' rookies went off to fight in WWII after the '41 season. Both were decorated with honors for their service. Who were the two Lions, and what honors did they receive?

17. How many players returned from the '41 season to play with Detroit the following year?

18. Before the 1942 season, the Lions held a scrimmage against the Army All-Stars. Proceeds of the game—$29,000—went to the Army Relief Fund. Who won the contest and by what score?

19. What did Bill Edwards do after his coaching stint with the Lions?

20. What was coach Jon Karcis' nickname?

21. What team record did Elmer Hackney establish against Pittsburgh on November 8, 1942?

22. How many times were the Lions shutout in 1942?

23. How many points did they yield during the course of that season?

24. Who led the team in receiving in 1941 and 1942?

25. How many passes did center-lineman-linebacker Alex Wojciechowicz catch in 1942?

26. What other function did Wojie serve for the team three times that year?

27. What was Gus Dorais's first name?

28. How long of a contract was Dorais originally given?

29. Where did Dorais play football in college?

30. According to football legend, Gus was responsible for making passing a legitimate offensive threat in a game against Army in 1913. He threw footballs to one of the game's legendary players and coaches. Who was Dorais's target in that famous game?

31. What was the significance of the game between the Lions and New York Giants on November 7, 1943?

32. Where did Frank Sinkwich play college ball?

33. Why was Sinkwich discharged from the Marines, allowing him to play football in '43?

34. How long after his discharge did he wait before playing with the Lions?

35. What award did he win after the '43 season?

36. After the season was completed, Frank enlisted in the U.S. Maritime Service. What was the reason for his discharge from the merchant marine?

37. In a game against the Bears on November 19, 1944, Sinkwich became the first Lions' passer to achieve what feat?

38. Who was the legendary Green Bay Packer that Sinkwich beat out for the 1944 league MVP honors?

39. Speaking about the Packers, Alex Wojciechowicz was a member of the "Seven Blocks of Granite" at Fordham that featured another legendary Packer. Who was this famous coach of the green-and-gold?

40. How many passes did Wojciechowicz intercept during the 1944 season?

41. Who was the Lions' top draft choice in 1944?

42. Two former Lions were killed while serving their country in 1944. Name these two heroes.

43. Who led the team in receiving 1945-47?

44. In a game against Green Bay on October 7, 1944, Don Hutson burned the Lions' secondary time and time again. How many touchdowns did he have in the second quarter of that game?

45. What Detroit Lions' guard returned from three years of service in World War II to gain All-League honors for the 1945 season?

46. What Lions' backfield star signed with Buffalo of the All-America Football Conference before the '46 season?

47. What was his nickname?

48. What future Lions' director of player personnel, executive vice-president, and general manager was drafted as a player by Detroit in 1946?

49. What team did Alex Wojciechowicz get traded to early in the 1946 season?

50. How long was Bill DeCorrevont's punt at Washington on October 6, 1946 during a 16-17 loss?

51. At 1-10, Detroit was one of only two NFL teams with losing records for the '46 season. Name the other team.

52. Who led the Lions in passing that year with 965 yards?

53. Who did the Lions give up to obtain the rights to Bill Dudley from the Pittsburgh Steelers?

54. How long did the Dudley deal take before it was done?

55. How much did Mandel pay Dudley in order to convince him to play?

56. What was Dudley's nickname?

57. What honor did Dudley win with the Steelers for the 1946 season?

58. What Heisman trophy winner from Army did Detroit draft in '47?

59. What was Dave Ryan's nickname?

60. Who led the team in passing in '47?

61. Who led the team in scoring?

62. Who did the Lions' players elect as team captain for that year?

63. How much did shares in the team stock sell for under new owners Fife and Anderson in 1948?

64. Bo McMillan was the owners' second choice for the job of head coach. Their first choice was the coach of Notre Dame at that time. Who was he?

65. What was Bo McMillan's first name?

66. How long of a contract did he sign?

67. This rookie quarterback was McMillan's choice to start for the Lions during the '48 season. Name him.

68. Who was the Lions' number one draft choice in '48?

69. What offensive lineman from the University of Illinois joined the team that same year?

70. Name the first two African-Americans to play on the Detroit Lions.

71. Who led the Lions with 450 receiving yards in '48?

72. Who led the team in rushing 1946-48?

73. Who had a total of six interceptions and led the Lions in that category for the 1948 season?

74. What famous Lions' receiver did McMillan obtain via a trade with the Washington Redskins in 1948?

75. At the time of the trade, this player was not a receiver. What position did he originally play?

76. Who holds the record for longest interception return for a touchdown (102 yards) in club history, set on November 24, 1949 against the Chicago Bears?

77. How many picks did this player have for the '49 season?

78. The answer to the previous question was not enough to lead the team that year. This distinction goes to Don Doll, who intercepted 11 passes in '49. Two of the picks were run back for scores. Doll set an NFL record in that same game on Oct. 23 against the Chicago Cardinals for most interceptions by one player in a single game. How many INT's did he snag in the game? (Incidentally, the Lions won the game, 24-7)

79. Who was appointed assistant to the general manager that year and would be instrumental in building the team that would lead Detroit into its golden era?

80. Bill Dudley led the Lions for a third straight year in scoring in '49. How many points did he score that year?

81. Who was the team's top draft choice in '49?

82. What team did this player get traded to that year?

83. What three quarterbacks shuffled in and out of the lineup during the year?

84. Who was the Lions' first 1,000-yard receiver for a single season?

85. How many receptions did he have that year?

What college or university did each play for?

86. Byron White

87. Lloyd Cardwell

88. Russell Thomas

89. Camp Wilson

90. Bob Mann

4
Life in the Fast Layne (1950-57)

Television had its Golden Age in the '50s with performers named Benny, Gleason, Ball—heck, Superman had his best days then—and with shows like *Father Knows Best, Dragnet, You Bet Your Life, Beat the Clock, Life of Riley, $64,000 Question, Toast of the Town*, to name some. There was even Howdy Doody and the Mickey Mouse Club for the kids. You couldn't see Elvis's gyrating hips, but just about everything else was on TV.

Coinciding with the glory days of the "idiot box," the Lions ushered in a Golden Age of their own, with a unique cast of stars, characters, rogues, and roughnecks. If they'd played prime-time, the program's title would have been, *The Greatest Show On Turf*, featuring Cloyce Box, Lou Creekmur, Leon Hart, Joe Schmidt, Doak Walker...

And starring Bobby Layne.

Bobby Layne arrived in Detroit at a time when fans and teammates were in a quandary. Several seasons of soul searching had ended in vain. Then Bobby Layne followed his destiny and became the team's kindred spirit. Nobody before or after would leave a more colorful impression. An imaginative free-lancer at the line of scrimmage, he was the nexus of one of the greatest football teams of all time. Sometimes he threw wounded ducks, but when he connected for a score or a big play to turn a game around, there was nothing more beautiful than Layne's frequently sore right arm. *Sports Illustrated* has called him the "toughest quarterback ever." He was the last player in the NFL to play without a face mask. He could jump down a teammate's throat one moment, then be slapping him on the back after the next play because the players responded to Bobby.

A better definition of Layne the player—and Layne the person—can be offered by remembering the Monday afternoon ritual he originated back in his heyday. Bobby would gather the team in the Stadium Bar for a private session of having fun and celebrating those better times. It was a means to unwind, to gloat over triumph or forget loss. It was a reason to party, which was as much Layne's pastime as football was his passion. Sometimes his off-field reputation preceded his accomplishments on the gridiron. It always kept him in the public eye, whether he was at the center of a bar brawl or cited for a traffic violation. He had as much disdain for curfews as an insolent teenager. Once in awhile, his erratic play would elicit boos from the Briggs Stadium faithful. But none of it deterred him from giving all of himself for the game or being able to rally his troops around him. For the most part, the Monday gatherings were a show of team unity and friendship; two elements that would help the Lions reach pro football immortality three times throughout the decade.

It began with the acquisition of key players. Bo McMillan drafted Heisman trophy winners Doak Walker and Leon Hart. He traded for Layne on April 26, 1950. The All-America Football Conference went into the history books in 1949, so the Lions obtained the services of Bob Smith, Lou Creekmur, and Bob Hoernschemeyer from the disbanded league.

All was not glorious the first year of the new era. Vast improvements were made in 1950, but the 6-6 record was not a reflection of the talent the team possessed. In the wake of the modest season, a member of the Lions' board of directors reportedly gathered Layne, Box, and Walker for a meeting. Discussions on the current direction of the team led to the coach's dismissal. Ironically, McMillan had been blackballed by the very players he had brought together in an effort to help the team win.

Buddy Parker was the heir of a killer nucleus. A shift in coaching attitudes, with more of an emphasis toward a free atmosphere was welcomed by the players. Practices on the field were usually reduced to under 90 minutes as opposed to the three-hour or longer sessions favored by McMillan. Discipline was harder to come by, but who could argue with a guy who was on the verge of winning two championships?

One thing Parker is often credited for installing in the psyche of NFL offenses is the now patented two-minute drill. According to Parker, at that time teams were not using the clock to their advantage just before the half and near the end of the game. Instead of slowing up or being content to let the remaining moments run down, he thought his team, guided by Layne's quick wits, could do plenty of damage when pressed by the clock. So the Lions repeatedly practiced this "brainchild" of Parker's, and Layne became a comeback artist.

Feeling that the Lions were only a couple of key players away from geatness, Parker made a shopping list of prospects. They would be moves designed to aid the team in a hurry, even if it meant giving up talent in the long run. Win now, worry about tomorrow later. That was Parker's philosophy.

Fullback appeared to be the position of greatest concern. Parker's solution was Pat Harder of the Chicago Cardinals, a hard hitting veteran whose best games were supposed to be from seasons past. Harder proved all the nay-sayers wrong and became an integral cog in the championship machines of '52 and '53. Other newcomers included future Hall-of-Famer Jack Christiansen and Dorne Dibble through the draft, and the versatile Jim Martin, who played linebacker-defensive lineman and kicker, from the Cleveland Browns.

At 7-4-1, the Lions were edged out in the West by the 8-4 Los Angeles Rams in 1951. By then, it was apparent that something great was in the works in Motown. Parker advertised that the Lions would be even better in 1952. Following their coach's lead, the players began making similar predictions.

To start the season, the Lions dropped two of their first three games. Both losses came at the hands of the team that sealed their doom on the last game of the year before, the San Francisco 49ers. Neither game was close. The season opener ended in a 17-3 score. A pitiful offensive performance during the rematch in Week Three convinced coach Parker to yank Layne. The game was an old fashioned shellacking. Changing quarterbacks did little to help as the Niners wound up 28-0 victors at Briggs Stadium. After the game, Parker went directly home to mull over the condition of his team. Concern over his job status and the welfare of the team prompted Layne to show up a while later and guarantee that he was the man who would straighten out the Lions and put them back on the winning track.

This was not evident in the first quarter of the next game, as the visiting Rams shot out to a 13-0 lead. But Layne never let the game slip away, showing the great poise of a leader that would nullify many deficits in his time. He connected with Cloyce Box on a 64-yard score, and the transformation had begun. Detroit ended up winning that game, 24-16. They rambled off eight wins out of the last nine games, a surge that carried them to a tie for the division title with the Los Angeles Rams. Both teams managed 9-3 marks.

Good news came to the Lions in time for the playoff game with Los Angeles. Doak Walker, who had missed most of 10 regular season games, was back. Pat Harder scored 19 points, and Walker threw a halfback option touchdown to Leon Hart to lead the Lions to a 31-21 win. Layne was unspectacular, but, as always, his knack for making the big play ignited the confidence of his fellow players.

In Cleveland the next week, Detroit relied heavily on Layne and Walker to win the championship. Both players scored touchdowns while leading the Lions to a 17-7 victory. With Bobby Layne coming of age, the Detroit Lions were the best football team on the planet.

Back-to-back championships were brought to the city of Detroit in 1953. The player who made the biggest impact that year and who would continue to be the heart of Lions' defenses for years to come was a rookie linebacker named Joe Schmidt. He would later coach the team and be named Mr. Detroit Lion in an area media poll conducted in 1993 in honor of 60 years of Detroit Lions football. Behind the driving force of Layne and Company on offense and the surges of Schmidt on defense, the Lions finished 10-2 for the season. They went on to beat Cleveland once again in the Championship game, 17-16.

A picture perfect example of Layne's football personality came in the third game of the season against San Francisco. The Lions had lost five in a row to the Niners. Bobby predicted that his team would score in two plays. He miscalculated by one. The Detroit offense moved the ball 72 yards for a touchdown on *three* plays. It sparked Detroit to a huge 24-21 win that set the stage for the season.

Almost equaling that impressive mark, the Lions of 1954 finished at 9-2-1 for their third straight Western Division title. Layne missed some action during the season with a sore shoulder, a concussion, and later, a broken nose. But he gutted it out when the team needed him most. The final game of the regular season was a prelude to the championship game one week later. On the snow-covered field of Cleveland Stadium, the Lions beat the Browns for the seventh time in a row under Buddy Parker. The score of the game was 14-10.

Long before the 1995 playoff disaster at Philadelphia, the Lions suffered their worst defeat in team history on December 26, 1954. Layne threw a playoff record six interceptions as Cleveland trounced the favored Lions, 56-10. Unforgiving Detroit fans hated Layne for blowing the Lions' chance at a three-peat. It was a resentment that would resurface time and time again.

Les Bingaman, a seven year standout at middle guard on defense, retired before the start of the 1955 season. In his absence, Parker switched from a five-man line to a new 4-3 scheme, in which Joe Schmidt would occupy the new middle linebacker position. The 4-3 would become a monster for defenses around the league, but the Lions struggled with it their first year.

Cloyce Box also retired. Making matters worse on offense was Layne's sore shoulder. The injury occurred in the off-season while his son was riding on a horse. After the horse turned wild, Bobby pulled hard on the reins in an effort to subdue the animal and strained his shoulder. He was never the same during the season, in which he later suffered a knee injury. The fierce competitor that he was, Layne stuck it out and endured a miserable campaign. The Lions fell to the bottom at 3-9. Included in the disastrous turnaround was a string of six losses to start the year.

Another retirement came after the season; this one more severe than those of the past year. Detroit said good-bye to then all-time scoring leader, Doak Walker. His backfield mate, Bob Hoernschemeyer, who led the team in rushing 1950-53, also retired. Their departures made a climb in the standings a bit more inclement. Heisman Trophy winner, Howar "Hopalong" Cassady was drafted to fill the void left by Walker, while Detroit also drafted Don McIlhenny to take over Hoernschemeyer's role.

A reversal was in order for the new season, and it started out just the way the Lions wanted it. An undefeated six-game start escalated to 9-2 by the time of the season finale in Chicago versus the 8-2-1 Bears. Ed Meadows blind-sided a relaxed Layne after a hand-off, and the QB was knocked cold. Lou Creekmur and Bill Bowman each took shots at Meadows to retaliate for their admired leader. That blow would end up costing Detroit another chance at the championship. Chicago won the game, 38-21. The loss would set in motion the incidents that would lead to Bobby's ticket out of town.

Layne's departure from the Lions was orchestrated after the arrival of veteran Packers QB, Tobin Rote. Buddy Parker felt that the team needed a second quarterback for insurance to such a calamity as happened in the Bears game. Rote was dealt to the Lions prior to training camp. It would be one of Parker's last deals for Detroit, a sort of exclamation point to his tenure. After being rewarded with a two-year extension at $30,000 per season, Buddy shocked the team at their annual "Meet the Lions" banquet on August 12, 1957, by calling it quits. He reasoned that he could not handle the team anymore and did not want to take part in another losing year, which he thought the Lions were destined for. Before the start of the regular season, Parker took the head coaching job at Pittsburgh.

Later in life, Buddy would claim that his decision to leave Detroit was the biggest mistake in his pro football career.

The owners' search for a new coach ended abruptly. They promoted assistant coach George Wilson to the vacant position. Wilson played revolving quarterbacks throughout the season, depending on which of the two had the hot hand at the moment. Of course, the two platoon system could not have worked. If Bobby was cold one quarter, he would be warming the bench without much of a chance to play through the rough spots. Why Wilson did not realize that to be a mistake is anybody's guess, but hadn't Bobby proven that he was the Great Redeemer? You never knew when he'd get the kinks out and turn adversity into momentum. Anyway, Wilson stuck with his philosophy. That is, until Bobby broke his ankle on a play against the Cleveland Browns. The pocket had collapsed, and Don Colo and Paul Wiggin nailed him. Layne was taken off the field on a stretcher.

With Layne on crutches, it was up to Rote to guide the Lions to a division title and win the respect of his new team. In two commanding performances, Rote led the Lions to victory in the Cleveland game, then, in the season finale in Chicago, he resurrected a dead first half Detroit offense to score three TDs for a 21-13 triumph. It was obvious that Rote had the necessary intangibles needed to be a successful quarterback. The Lions were in good hands.

Next came a post-season showdown with the 49ers to determine the Western Division champs. Both teams finished at 8-4. Falling behind, 27-7, in the third quarter, the Lions' fate seemed to be sealed. But the team fielded by Wilson that day had a burning desire to feel the glory of another championship, and a miraculous finish was in the works. With Rote's precision passing and the running of Tom Tracy, Detroit scored three touchdowns in under five minutes and added a field goal later in the game to steal the division title by a score of 31-28.

The pinnacle of Tobin Rote's success came during the championship game in Cleveland. He chose his plays effectively in conducting the Lions to a big lead early on. Support for Rote was growing with every snap. By the end of the 59-14 rout, Tobin Rote had made believers out of the 55,000-plus at Briggs Stadium.

Rote's popularity with the town had eclipsed Layne's.

Layne had reached the end of the line after two poor performances to start the 1958 season. Faced with the problem of having two starters worthy of playing time, coach Wilson sided with the growing sentiment of the fans and opted for Rote.

"Tobin's the one that won it for us," Wilson told the team.

After the deal was done, sending Layne to Parker's Pittsburgh Steelers, Wilson said he chose Bobby as expendable, "because I would have been run out of town if we traded Rote."

It was true that Layne's heroics were not cherished long by some of the fans back then. He would win a game one week, then be the scapegoat the next if they lost. But he played with a reckless abandon and lived life to its fullest in the same way. He was a genuine character whose style of play was infectious.

Bobby Layne and his teammates won a lot of games, and he made sure they had fun. He later recalled that the thing he missed most about his football days was his teammates. He missed rousing around with them and identifying with them.

That says it all as to why the unceremonious exodus of their inspired leader provoked frustration and resentment from Lions players. It brought tears to the eyes of grown men.

After all, Bobby Layne was the beating heart of Detroit Lions' football.

TRIVIA QUESTIONS

The Golden Age Quiz
1. What team was Bobby Layne traded from to Detroit?

2. Who did Detroit originally trade away in the Layne deal?

3. The player in the last question refused to be traded. Who did the Lions send in his place?

4. Which player was given a screen test by Universal Pictures prior to coming to Detroit?

5. Along with the trades that brought Layne and Box to Detroit, Bo McMillan acquired other key players for the Lions before his dismissal. Name the teams these players came from.
    1.) Ollie Cline
    2.) Dick Flanagan
    3.) John Prchlik
    4.) Jim Cain

6. What two AAC teams did Bob Hoernschemeyer play for prior to becoming a Lion?

7. Buddy Parker had quit as coach of what NFL team before coming

to Detroit as Bo McMillan's backfield aid?

8. What was Thurman McGraw's nickname?

9. How many seasons did he play for Detroit?

10. What team was Bill Dudley traded to in January 1950?

11. In a game on October 29, 1950 against the LA Rams, what Lions' player set a then NFL mark by accumulating 331 total yards during the contest?

12. Who set a Lions record with a 96-yard run against the New York Yanks on November 23, 1950?

13. In a game against the first Baltimore Colts team (they would disband at the end of the 1950 season, and a completely different Baltimore Colts franchise would move to the city in 1953) on December 3, 1950, Cloyce Box caught 12 passes and scored 3 TDs. He came up one yard short of the then all-time single game record for receiving yards. How many yards did he have for the game?

14. How many receptions did Box have during the 1950 season?

15. He finished second in the NFL in that category for the season. What player from the Rams finished ahead of him for the league lead?

16. Which Lions player won the scoring title with 128 points as a rookie in 1950?

17. Who set a franchise record for most interceptions in a single year during that season?

18. What high school football team did Layne and Walker play on together?

19. What was Buddy Parker's first name?

20. How long was Parker's original contract when he was hired as head coach?

21. What was Bob Hoernschemeyer's nickname?

22. What three players did the Lions lose to the armed services before the start of the 1951 season?

23. Who did Detroit trade to the Cardinals for Pat Harder?

24. What Cleveland Browns fullback was Parker's first choice before he dealt for Harder?

25. Paul Brown, the Cleveland coach, told Parker he could have this player and one of the Browns' first string tackles. Who did Brown want?

26. The Lions lost their 1951 first round pick to a knee injury the player suffered in training camp. Who was he?

27. This player set a record by returning four punts for TDs in a season in 1951. Who is he?

28. With Cloyce Box gone for the season, who led the team in receptions for 1951?

29. How many TD passes did Layne throw that year?

30. Former tackle Russ Thomas, whose career ended from a knee injury, took over what function for the Lions in 1952?

31. What nickname did Pat Harder pick up that year?

32. Why did he receive this nickname?

33. What round was Yale Lary selected in during the 1952 draft?

34. What round was Jim David drafted in?

35. How many seasons did he play for the Lions?

36. Doak Walker cut his right arm on a broken car window and was sidelined for the '52 pre-season. What major sporting event was he attending when he sustained the injury?

37. Who did Parker trade for to take Walker's place?

38. What team did this player come from? What position did he play for his former team?

39. What was this player's actual first name?

40. Going into the '52 season, Parker felt it necessary to have a quality backup for Layne. What former Chicago Cardinal did he acquire for second string?

41. Who became the Lions' defensive co-ordinator in '52?

42. The Lions had to give up a player in order to acquire the aforementioned co-ordinator from the Chicago Cardinals. Who was the player and what were the odd circumstances behind the deal?

43. What team held the potent Lions offense to only four first downs and a total of 65 yards on October 12, 1952?

44. How many points did the Lions score against the Green Bay Packers on October 26, 1952, to set a franchise record for most points in a regular season game?

45. What team did the Lions hold to 3 yards rushing on November 9, 1952?

46. Doak Walker was able to return from an injury on December 7 of that same year in a game against the Chicago Bears, but coach Parker was careful not to overuse him. Walker's replacement, Girard, was out for the season, and Bob Hoernschmeyer had injured ribs. In the game, who led the Lions' ground attack with a touchdown and 54 rushing yards?

47. Cloyce Box returned from a year of service in the marines in 1952 and set a new team record. What was the record?

48. Who was voted the Lions' MVP in '52?

49. What was the title given to the award for team MVP?

50. The Lions first game after the 1952 championship was an exhibition game that they won, 24-10. Who were the Lions' opponents in the game played at Chicago's Soldiers Field.

51. Who was the Lions' first round pick in the 1953 college draft?

52. How many rookies made the roster to start the 1953 season?

53. The emergence of rookie Joe Schmidt that year prompted coach Parker to trade away one of the team's more popular players to Pittsburgh. Who was the player?

54. This Lions rookie scored on a 73-yard punt return the first time he ever touched the ball in an NFL game. Who was he?

55. This Lions rookie also scored the first time he touched the ball, a one-yard plunge on the way to a victory over the Pittsburgh Steelers on September 27, 1953. Who was he?

56. What Lions player became a villain in the hearts of San Francisco fans for breaking Y. A. Tittle's jaw in a 1953 game?

57. The player in the answer to the last question was also pegged as a villain for a play in Los Angeles the following week. What Rams player was injured in the play?

58. By what name was the Lions' secondary called throughout most of the '50s?

59. Jack Christiansen tied a team mark for interceptions in a season during 1953. How many did he have for the year?

60. How many INTs did the Lions have as a team that year to lead the league?

61. What team was Don Doll traded to?

62. Long before Bo Jackson or Deion Sanders did it, these three Lions teammates played a season of both football and baseball in 1953. Name them.

63. Pat Harder retired after 1953. He later came back to the NFL as a non-player. What job did he take with the league?

64. Defensive middle guard Les Bingaman showed up overweight to training camp in 1954, sparking a bet between Parker and defensive coach Buster Ramsey. They bet a steak on who was closer guessing Bingaman's weight. Parker guessed the lineman would weigh closer to 400 pounds, while Ramsey said it would be closer to 300. Who won the bet?

65. What two Lions were lost for the 1954 season while serving military duty?

66. What player was involved in a fight and lost a tooth in Ann Arbor one night in '54 causing coach Parker to institute an 11:30 p.m. curfew during training camp?

67. What Lions rookie returned a kick 100 yards for a TD in the '54 season opening victory against the Chicago Bears?

68. Why was the regular season game in Cleveland on October 3, 1954 moved to December 19 and played a week after the regular season was to have ended?

69. Who was Buddy Parker referring to when he said: "It was the greatest performance I've seen in coaching?"

70. Against the Rams on October 10, 1954, who played quarterback for an injured Bobby Layne?

71. What team did the Lions tie 13-13 on December 5, 1954?

72. Who led the team in receiving in 1954?

73. The Lions lost Cloyce Box, Thurman McGraw, and Les Bingaman to retirement in 1955. Another player jumped to the Canadian Football League and would not return to the Lions. Who was he?

74. Who called signals on defense for the Lions throughout the mid-'50s to early '60s?

75. Who led the Lions in rushing in 1955?

76. What position was Leon Hart converted to for the season of '56?

77. Who led the Lions in rushing that year?

78. What player led the team in receiving in '55 and '56?

79. What team did George Wilson once play for?

80. How old was Wilson when he took over the head coaching job for

Detroit?

81. What player was obtained from San Francisco for Bill Bowman and Bill Stitz prior to the 1957 season?

82. What two players were Oliver Spencer, Jim Salisbury, Norm Masters, and Don McIlhenny traded for?

83. Who led the team in rushing in 1957?

84. What was the compensation value from Pittsburgh for Bobby Layne?

What numbers did these players wear?

85. Bobby Layne

86. Doak Walker

87. Cloyce Box

88. Bob Hoernschemeyer

89. Joe Schmidt

90. Leon Hart

91. Yale Lary

92. Jack Christiansen

93. Les Bingaman

94. Jim David

Name the college or university each played for:

95. Pat Harder

96. Cloyce Box

97. Les Bingaman

98. Jim David

99. Bob Hoernschmeyer

100. Leon Hart

5
Mad Duck But No Glory
(1958-70)

he remnants of the Bobby Layne legend were dusted off the spirit of the team and swept away to Pittsburgh on October 6, 1958, but the emotional ties lingered on and the Lions played with a lack of conviction throughout the remainder of a 4-7-1 year. Another losing season followed (3-8-1) to close out the Lions' greatest decade on a sour note. The Tobin Rote experiment had failed after a two-year trial. Out of disparity from both sides, the fan favorite played out his contract, then moved onto the Canadian Football League.

Despite the loss of Layne, there was a new hope dawning over the horizon. The departure of one character in Detroit made room for another. Looking at Alex Karras on the sideline, one would have thought he was more Baby Huey than "Mad Duck", but the latter was what they called him because of his intense, quick choreography on the gridiron. Off the field, he had a joking, lively manner that would foster itself into an acting career once the game was over. He was a mean s.o.b. down in the trenches, though, improvising in any fashion, clean or dirty, in order to sack a quarterback or dismantle a run. Drafted in 1958, he played the game mostly blind without the aid of his thick glasses, but he had a sixth sense on the football field. Baltimore Colts running back Lenny Moore once commented on Alex's speed: "Running away from Karras is worse than running at him."

A prime example of Karras's spirit and mentality came in 1967, after the NFL-AFL merger. It was a pre-season game in Denver that pitted the Lions against the old AFL Broncos. No NFL team wanted to be the first to lose to an AFL team. It would be as disgraceful as a boy getting a black eye from a girl. Upstart Denver had no idea they were supposed to be trounced. They began boasting that they would break the win barrier against the Lions. Karras was provoked. He promised that he would walk back to Detroit if the Lions lost. Well, the Broncos made history that day by a 13-6 margin, and Karras was in no mood to make good on his vow when he boarded the team bus after the defeat. He hated losing.

An aggressive defense that featured Roger Brown, Sam Williams, and Darris McCord next to Karras, Joe Schmidt in the middle, and Yale Lary and Dick "Night Train" Lane in the secondary took the Lions to three consecutive second place finishes. They would leave a legacy of one of the most dominant displays of defense in NFL history on November 11, 1962. Against the eventual champion Packers, Karras and Company ate alive Green Bay quarterback Bart Starr. 11 sacks were registered by the Lions' D during the 26-14 victory , the only defeat suffered by the Packers that year. It was the Lions' greatest year for victories up to that time, but eleven of them was not enough to overtake the Pack.

Detroit played in the short lived Playoff Bowl in 1960, 1961, and 1962. It was a showcase of divisional runners-up, a kind of consolation prize that said, "No, not quite good enough this year." The Lions went undefeated in their three appearances, knocking off past nemesis Cleveland the first year, then battering Philadelphia and Pittsburgh the next two. With a slew of talent, the Lions seemed on the verge of another great decade. Of course, looks can be deceiving.

There was another turnover in the front office early in the decade. The fight over control between former president D. Lyle Fife and president Edwin J. Anderson swelled until Anderson resigned as part of a compromise that was iinstituted to end the bickering. Anderson stayed on as general manager, while one of the stockholders, William Clay Ford, grandson of Henry Ford, succeeded him as president of the club. A couple of years later, Ford would buy out all stock from the remaining shareholders and become sole owner of the Detroit Lions.

An incident that quickly gained notoriety happened after the 1962 season. Karras, Green Bay legend Paul Hornung, and little known Ray Pearson were suspended by league commissioner Pete Rozelle for betting on NFL games. Five other Lions' players were fined $2,000 each for placing $50 wagers on the Packers-Giants championship game of 1962. The players penalized were Joe Schmidt, linebacker Wayne Walker, defensive end Sam Williams, defensive back Gary Lowe, and guard John Gordy. In addition, the Lions' organization was slapped with a $4,000 fine for coach Wilson's failure to report to authorities that certain players had associated with "known hoodlums," as the Detroit Police Department referred to them, and that the team had issued unauthorized people sideline passes. Karras and Hornung were reinstated after sitting out the full year.

1963 was a lost year without Karras. The Lions plummeted to fourth place with a 5-8-1 record. This was a team soon to be stripped of any delusions of a near-future run at a title.

Mediocrity followed for five seasons as troubles accumulated throughout those years. One of the biggest was the front office's failure to sign draft picks, though the track record indicates that the demand may have exceeded the effort. Many chose to play for the AFL, and a couple joined the Canadian Football League. Another thorn in the Lions' paw was an unresolved quarterback controversy. Milt Plum had been acquired in 1962 to save the offense but was benched every now and then in favor of Earl Morral. After Wilson resigned as coach on December 23, 1964, Morral was traded by new coach Harry Gilmer to the New York Giants. So Plum, finally lodged as the starter, spent the next couple of years as a sporadic field general. He would fizzle as frequently as he impressed. He went down in 1966 with a mid-season knee injury and found himself caught up in another mini-controversy with Karl Sweetan when he returned.

Tragedy made its presence felt during those years as well. Offensive tackle Lucien Reeberg died of heart failure due to toxic poisoning in his blood on January 31, 1964. Reeberg was a two year veteran who had been maturing into a good blocker. But his weight was an obstacle to his progress. He soon weighed slightly over 300 pounds. At the team's urging, he had been checked into the Detroit Osteopathic Hospital and placed on a weight reduction program. But it was too late. Reeberg was just 21 years old when he died.

Some personnel moves backfired. For instance, let me offer up the name Joe Don Looney. He had been a bull running the ball for the Baltimore Colts, but his reputation preceded him. What the Lions got in the trade with Baltimore was a bust. Looney skipped a practice, got into trouble with the police, and was inactive for most of the '65 season. The next year he was suspended for refusing to go into action in a game against the expansion Atlanta Falcons. He was subsequently traded away to the Washington Redskins.

Gilmer never worked out as head coach. Most of the players despised him. Enthusiasm from the front office had leveled off much the same way. After the '65 season, Joe Schmidt suggested that he had been fed up with the coach. Enough so to call it quits from the playing field. Nick Pietrosante, the team's leading rusher for three years in the early '60s, was put on waivers by Gilmer. The coach himself later admitted that he had made a mistake by keeping Plum over Morral. He was fired on January 5, 1967.

Through it all, the Lions struggled for respectability on the field. They finished 7-5-2 in 1964 and dropped to 6-7-1 the next season. They battled through an ugly 4-9-1 season in 1966 and did not get any prettier at 5-7-2 the year after. 1968 was just as bad. Detroit wound up 4-8-2.

Prospects began looking up as early as 1967. After Gilmore was let go, future Hall-of-Famer Joe Schmidt was hired as head coach. He would show as much tenacity running the team as he had in shaking off blockers. Two superstars came aboard. Mel Farr was Mr. Everything on offense, leading the team in rushing and becoming a scoring and receiving threat. Before Deion, there was Lem Barney. Only Lem didn't need to dance after a big play for added attention, and he could tackle. Barney set an NFL record by stealing 10 passes his rookie year.

Another gifted player made his debut in 1968. Charlie Sanders was the best tight end Detroit has ever had. Defenses couldn't cover him, so for the most part, they tried mugging him. He still managed to be a force over the middle and in the end zone.

Repeating history, Detroit initiated another QB controversy by trading for Bill Munson and drafting Greg Landry in the same year. The two of them juggled playing time, and the offense suffered from a lack of continuity. Quarterback controversies would be something that would dog the Lions for nearly 25 years to come.

Under Schmidt, though, the Lions had a good team. 1969 began a string of second place finishes. Though Alex Karras was still somewhat productive, the once vaunted defense was falling apart. Retirements, age, injuries all played a part in the decline. There was some new blood. The anchor was the mobile Mike Lucci at middle linebacker, a guy who knew how to thwart the run. Schmidt took up the job of personally tutoring him, and Lucci was a formidable heir-apparent to the man who defined the position. Paul Naumoff, another body pressing tackler, played beside Lucci. Of course, Lem Barney continued to electrify the league with his acrobatic picks and super-glue coverage. Meanwhile, on the line of scrimmage, Ed Flanagan was holding his own against the likes of Dick Butkus of the Bears and Minnesota's famous Fearsome Foursome. Detroit was back on the winning track at 9-4-1.

A 40-0 blowout of the Green Bay Packers kicked off the 1970 season. Bill Munson threw three touchdowns in the game, and Greg Landry scored another on a 76-yard sneak. After a quick 5-1 start, the Lions were defeated three times in a row. They were in jeopardy of losing position for a playoff berth. Because of the AFL-NFL's final merger, the playoff derby had been expanded to include two wild card teams. Some of the veterans sensed that this could be their swan song. Hungry for 13 years now, the Lions surged with a 5-0 run at season's end to qualify for a wild card spot.

The celebration was short lived. Whether or not the offense was crippled by jet lag after the flight to Dallas the players only know, but whatever the case was, the game turned out to be an epic struggle of defense on both sides of the ball. The Cowboys defense won the brawl, sealing Landry in his own end zone for a safety, and forcing crucial turnovers. A Dallas field goal was the only offensive points scored in the game. The Cowboys marched off the field with a 5-0 victory, thus slamming the door on any dreams Alex Karras and his team had of finally winning a championship.

Before the start of the season in 1971, it was evident to every one involved with the franchise that age had slowed down Mad Duck. No longer was he the dominant quarterback hunter of his glory years. Karras was placed on waivers, bringing an end to the 12-season career of the player who had been the epitome of one of the most ferocious defenses ever known to the NFL. Coach Schmidt said it was the toughest thing he ever had to do.

It was the closing of another era in Motown.

TRIVIA QUESTIONS

1958-70

1. What was Alex Karras's middle name?

2. Where was Karras born on July 15, 1935?

3. What high school in his home town was he an All-State fullback at?

4. What university did he play for?

5. What award did Karras win in 1957 as college football's outstanding lineman?

6. Besides Mad Duck, his incredible agility earned him another nickname. What was it?

7. During his suspension for gambling in 1963, what jobs did Alex hold?

8. Name the situation comedy Alex starred in during the '80s on ABC.

9. Alex Karras and his second wife, Susan Clark (who also starred on the TV series mentioned in the previous answer) started their own film production company. What did they name the company?

10. This star defensive back, who would play 14 seasons in Detroit, was picked up off the Cleveland Browns waiver wire. Who was he?

11. How many INTs did he have for his career with Detroit?

12. In 1958, Lions general manager, Nick Kerbawy, was lost to another pro sports team. What franchise did Kerbawy become GM at?

13. What two players participated in the longest kickoff return in team history (104 yards) during a 41-21 victory over the LA Rams on October 26, 1958?

14. What Canadian football team signed Tobin Rote?

15. What team traded Dick "Night Train" Lane to Detroit?

16. Who was traded by Detroit for Lane?

17. What team did Jim David become an assistant coach for after his career with Detroit?

18. What round was Roger Brown taken in during the 1960 Draft?

19. What round was Gail Cogdill drafted in that same year?

20. Who broke Ace Gutowsky's single season rushing record with 872 yards in 1960?

21. What legendary football coach became the Lions defensive backs coach in 1960?

22. In a gutsy performance six days after his eight-month-old son Michael died of leukemia, what Lions player booted three field goals, including a 49-yard game winner in a 16-14 victory over Baltimore on September 24, 1961?

23. The 1962 Draft was held in November of 1961 due to the war against the AFL. The first two players selected by Detroit went to the AFL anyway. Who were they?

24. In the trade for Milt Plum, the Lions also acquired running back Tommy Watkins and linebacker Dave Lloyd. Who did the Lions give the Browns?

25. On December 9, 1962, the Lions set a team record for takeaways against Minnesota. How many did they register during the game?

26. What TV show was Alex Karras a guest on when he admitted to betting on football in January 1963?

27. What two Lions receivers scored a combined 23 TDs in 1963?

28. He averaged 48.9 yards a punt in 1963, a team record. Who is he?

29. Name the player chosen in the 1964 Draft who opted for the Dallas Texans of the AFL.

30. Who did William Clay Ford appoint as director of player personnel after purchasing the team?

31. What round was Lucien Reeberg drafted in?

32. What college did he play for?

33. Why was he dropped from this school's team as a senior?

34. What Lions broadcaster coined the term "Fearsome Foursome"?

35. What Lions players were the "Fearsome Foursome"?

36. True or False? Alex Karras's brother Ted played for the Lions?

37. Who was drafted by Detroit in the third round of the '65 Draft?

38. What round was Karl Sweetan drafted in during that same draft?

39. What Green Bay tight end was obtained for the Lions #1 draft choice in '66?

40. What position had Harry Gilmer played when he was on the Lions roster in 1955-56?

41. Before becoming head coach of the Lions, Gilmer was an assistant coach. What team was that for?

42. Who did the Baltimore Colts obtain from Detroit for Joe Don Looney?

43. What reason did Looney give for not going back into the game against Atlanta that led to his suspension?

44. Who did Gilmer name team captain?

45. What team was Sam Williams traded to after the '65 season?

46. Why was Gail Cogdill suspended by Gilmer during the off-season in 1966?

47. What left-footed, soccer-style kicker joined the club mid-season in '66?

48. How many field goals did he kick in a game against Minnesota on November 13, 1966?

49. What team was Roger Brown traded to?

50. How old was Joe Schmidt when he took over as head coach on January 11, 1967?

51. Who were Schmidt's offensive assistants during his tenure as head coach?

52. Who did Joe hire to coach the defense?

53. Name the Lion receiver who totaled 1,266 yards receiving in 1966?

54. What round was defensive back Mike Weger drafted in 1967?

55. What future Lions kicker booted two field goals in Denver's upset over Detroit to become the first AFL team ever to beat an NFL team?

56. He scored on a 45-yard pass play the first time he touched the ball in the NFL against Buffalo in a pre-season game. Name him.

57. In the 1967 season opener against Green Bay, he scored a 24-yard TD the first time he touched the ball. Name him.

58. Who did the Lions get from the Rams for Milt Plum, Tommy Watkins, and Pat Studstill?

59. What incident led coach Schmidt to walk out on the team in 1968?

60. Who scouted Greg Landry and recommended that the Lions draft him?

61. What team record was set on September 22, 1968, during a 42-0 drubbing of the Bears?

62. Who was Russ Thomas referring to when he called a Chicago Bears player "an annihilating s.o.b.," after a game in which the Bears player poked Charlie Sanders in the eye after tackling him?

63. What two Lions players were selected to the NFL All-1960s team?

64. This Heisman Trophy winning running back was drafted by the

Lions in 1970. Name him.

65. This Saints kicker converted a 63-yard field goal against the Lions to give New Orleans a 19-17 victory on November 8, 1970. It still stands as the longest field goal in NFL history. Who kicked the field goal?

66. What team claimed Alex Karras off of waivers?

What college or university did each play for?

67. Nick Pietrosante

68. Darris McCord

69. Mel Farr

70. Milt Plum

71. Pat Studstill

72. Mike Lucci

73. Garo Yepremian

74. Joe Don Looney

75. Gail Cogdill

76. Terry Barr

What number did these players wear?

77. Nick Pietrosante

78. Mel Farr

79. Milt Plum

80. Mike Lucci

81. Gail Cogdill

6
LOOK HOMEWARD, LEO
(1971-79)

"Step right up and get your tickets while they're hot. Doesn't matter if there'll be rain sleet or snow, 'cause the show will go on. We'll just build a roof over your head."

No, that's not a pushy game day scalper, or the punch lines to a joke cracked by a Packer fan. It could have worked as an advertisement for the Detroit Lions, though, circa 1975. An invitation for the fans to become dome dwellers.

Just the idea of the Pontiac Silverdome and its brethren facilities around the league starts up a fundamental debate. Grass versus carpet. Chance of wind and an uncompromising precipitation factor outdoors versus a weather controlled climate indoors. A 70-degree temperature in December?

Purists will scoff at any attempt to alter the way football is played as taking a sledge hammer to the game and denting the concept. Well, if we stuck with the infant version, football's stone age if you will, nobody would be watching the plethora of exciting 6-3 games, or better yet, the handfuls of 0-0 deadlocks. Their arguments when it comes to domed stadiums is well taken. They would have the average fan believe its not football unless played on a natural surface where the elements are as much a part of the game as hot dog vendors and Gatorade showers for coaches. To some, dome field advantage is an added dimension to the game. The loud, raucous environment serves as the 12th man down on the field, more so than an open air stadium. Mother Nature simply is not admitted to the game. The only worries facing the teams are their opponents and injuries. Besides, the facility can accommodate some 80,000 fans.

I guess that was the intention.

Whichever way you look at it, the Pontiac Silverdome is home-sweet-home for the Detroit Lions. It's part of their history. Over the years, it has become as big a part of Lions tradition as Briggs Stadium was for fans in the '40s and '50s.

So what is the story behind the dome?

During the early years, the biggest concern for the Detroit Lions was drawing a decent fan base to perpetuate the life of the club. It did not take the team long to outgrow its humble beginnings.

Success and a colorful fashion of play in the '50s kept the Lions in newspapers all over the country, but the popularity of professional football itself had reached new heights with the advent of television. Since the Lions fielded one of the best squads in those days, their own popularity exploded. The next dozen years or so brought quality teams that achieved near misses at glory. If anything was constant, the crowds were getting larger; thus, the stadium began to seem smaller and smaller...

It was time to move.

Tiger Stadium had room for one team. A baseball team. The Tigers had their offices in the stadium, while the Lions' offices were on Michigan Avenue. Another inconvenience for the Lions was not being able to practice on the field during the baseball season. How could the Lions be pushy about the matter, considering the ball park was the original home to and later re-named after the baseball club?

The itch to move began as early as the 1950s. Many plans for a new facility were hatched over the years as the Lions played on at Tiger Stadium. One of the earliest plans came out of an effort to bring the Olympic games to the area. The city proposed a new stadium to be built at the State Fairgrounds, to be called Olympic Stadium. It was believed at that time that the capacity of such a complex would be a staggering 100,000 seats. That might have been fine for an international event, but a football team, more than likely, would have drowned in the expanse. Reluctance by the Olympic committee in considering Detroit as a site for the games killed that possibility. Instead, a smaller 80,000-seat stadium, to be built at the same site, was offered to the Lions. Again, the plan fell through.

Then the city's commissioners began talking about a site along the Detroit River. That plan would have worked, minus one minor detail. The Lions organization was firm on its stance to build near Tiger Stadium, or on secondary locations on Michigan Avenue or north of the Fisher Freeway. Owner William Clay Ford desired an 80,000-seat stadium, and, being an astute business mind, he realized a riverfront site would not garner the necessary revenue needed to pay off his dream stadium. Nor did he like the traffic and parking dilemmas he envisioned for the crowded area. The commission would not allow a new complex to be built in the vicinity of Tiger Stadium, so the two sides were at a standstill. Incidentally, Joe Louis Arena was later built near the Detroit River.

Ford was not about to let the commission bully him into accepting their proposal, but he was not about to pull what fans nowadays would call an Art Modell and transfer the franchise a few states over. The only apparent solution was to move the team to a nearby location outside the city.

Residents of Pontiac voted to finance the construction of a new stadium on December 11, 1972. Delays ensued over funding, but by September of '73, the hurdles were cleared and the project was underway. Ground at the intersection of Opdyke and M-59 was chosen as the location.

By the time it opened for business at the beginning of the 1975 season, the stadium was a state of the art facility with a capacity slightly over 80,000. Ford had his dream stadium, and Lions fans had room enough to bring their friends. After 40-plus years of historic football, the Detroit Lions had a place they could call their own.

On the field before the move, tragedy had been a double-edged sword for the Lions. In a game against the Chicago Bears on October 24, 1971, the Tiger Stadium crowd was stunned and silent after wide receiver Chuck Hughes collapsed to the grass while on his way back to the team huddle. Hughes had just finished running his route and everything seemed normal. It was a 28-23 score in favor of the Bears, and Detroit was mounting a last ditch effort to pull out a victory. With 62 seconds remaining in the game, Chuck Hughes suffered a heart attack.

The image of that day still remains: Hughes face down, motionless on the turf, and Dick Butkus of the Bears frantically waving his arms toward the Lions' bench. Team doctors worked on reviving him, but all efforts of resuscitation were unsuccessful. One hour later at the Henry Ford Hospital, Chuck Hughes was pronounced dead at the age of 28, the only man ever to pass away on a pro football field.

The 1971 season was never the same. Detroit had chances to make a run at the playoffs but folded in the final three weeks and fell out of contention at 7-6-1.

A fourth straight second place finish accompanied an 8-5-1 mark in 1972. The Lions, particularly coach Scmidt, believed that they could have won the division over the Packers, but failed in a key game at Green Bay late in the year, 33-7. Detroit had a potent offense with Greg Landry coming around and Charlie Sanders snagging any ball in sight, not to mention a top running game and one of the best offensive lines in the league, but the defense was a glaring weakness. The pass rush had done a disappearing act since the times of Alex Karras and Company.

1972 will be remembered as the year the Lions said good-bye to long time hero Joe Schmidt. It has often been said that he is the epitome of the Detroit Lions, whether playing hard and motivating those around him, or holding a team together through adversity, the way he did when he was a coach. The latter portion of his career ended when he stepped down from the post after season's end.

Don McCafferty was called on to replace the legend. He guided Detroit to yet another second place finish in '73. One of the team's main crutches the past few years had been their inability to beat the Vikings. It was a streak that had climbed to 10 defeats in a row entering the season. True to form, they dropped the two yearly contests to Minnesota and conceded the division to the Vikings by five and a half games. The subpar year—6-7-1—provoked owner Ford to question his team. "I don't think they want to win," he said. "At least, it doesn't look like it."

McCafferty's coaching style was more laid back than the players had been used to. If anything, his most obvious fault was his tendency to air out his frustrations to the media, but the players had slowly begun to grow comfortable with his business-like demeanor. It appeared that he had the team turned in the right direction.

Sadly, a heart attack ended Don McCafferty's life on July 28, 1974. Assistant Rick Fortano was elevated to head coach. The second tragedy in less than two years sent the Lions reeling through the first four games of the year. Only a late surge could salvage the season. All seven wins came in the final 10 games to secure a .500 record. Bill Munson, who had wrested the starting job from Greg Landry in the pre-season, separated his shoulder and lost hard earned playing time back to the former Number 1 pick. A slight moral victory was achieved on October 20 when the Lions finally beat the Vikings, 20-16, to end their drought of losses to the Purple People Eaters at an unlucky 13.

Playing in a new home did not supply the Lions with any extra inspiration. At a repeat of 7-7, the team failed to pull itself out of second place in 1975. It was now seven years running as Central Division runner-up. The offense was stunted by injuries to both quarterbacks. Defense was on the upswing. A prominent newcomer in the lineup was 245-pound tackle Doug English who would star for the defensive squad through the rest of the decade and into the early '80s.

Fortano resigned four games into his second season, but more than likely would have been the recipient of Ford's sharpened ax anyway. The club was 1-3 at the time and in dire need of an overhaul. Anything that would give them momentum to get over the hump. On October 5, 1976, two days after losing, 24-14, at Green Bay, Tommy Hudspeth was tabbed interim head coach. So basically, the Lions' former co-ordinator of personnel and scouting was awarded the job on a trial-and-error basis, with the team's play during the remainder of the season being what ultimately held his fate in the balance.

The offensive attack employed by him in his head coaching debut responded by rolling over the formidable New England Patriots' defense. A 30-10 win impressed the organization and pumped life into the fans. Due to a suspect line, however, the offense ceased to exist when under duress. A 41-point output in a victory over Seattle was offset by a meager seven points the week before in Washington, and it was followed by a spell of four games in which the Lions mustered final scores in the teens. An even 5-5 record justified a contract extension for the coach.

The offense during the 1977 season continued its trend of resembling an unfaithful car. Once in a while, you could count on it getting you somewhere, and other times, especially when you needed it most, it stalled. Heck, the engine never cranked over during a 37-0 route at the hands of the Dallas Cowboys, but she purred like a kitten in a 20-0 victory over the San Diego Chargers the week after. A banged up squad, particularly the running backs, was another reason for the year's struggles. A season finale defeat to the rival Vikings, 21-30, did not bolster Hudspeth's standing. He was fired on January 9, 1978, as the result of a 6-8 record and countless lackluster performances by his personnel.

It was becoming increasingly apparent that someone was needed to light a fire in the belly of the team. The torch bearer was two years away yet.

Monte Clarke came aboard as head coach in 1978. One of the major changes issued by the league for that season was an extension of the regular season from 14 games to 16. Aiding offenses, a five-yard "chucking" rule was enforced, in which receivers could not be touched by defenders five yards beyond the line of scrimmage. The previous rule allowed contact up to the point that the pass was released. For the Lions, a key change came when an aging, banged up Landry was replaced at QB by Gary Danielson after the fifth game. Danielson showed hints that he was the quarterback of the future, as he directed the team to six of the season's seven wins.

Then came the drop. At 2-14, the Lions practically fell off the face of the football world in '79. This was even more of an embarrassment, considering Detroit had been tagged by many as pre-season favorites to win the NFC Central division. Danielson's knee injury during the final pre-season contest caused the offense to shut down. With the defense unable to pick up the slack, it was Detroit's worst season in forty years.

But the Lions were the number one team. At least for the upcoming NFL Draft, anyway. It was a gift well received, as the opposition would soon find out.

TRIVIA QUESTIONS

1971-79

1. Chuck Hughes played two seasons with Detroit. What team had he played three seasons with before he was a Lion?

2. What was Hughes's nickname?

3. What famous golfer was a close friend of Hughes?

4. What Lion scored on a 102-yard kickoff return against Chicago on October 24, 1971?

5. He also returned a kickoff for a TD against Atlanta on October 3, 1971. How long was the score?

6. Who became the Lions' first 1,000-yard rusher in 1971?

7. Where did he rank for the season in that category for NFC rushers with 1,035?

8. How many rushing TDs did he score for the year?

9. Greg Landry set an NFL record at that time for the most running yards by a QB in one season. How many rushing yards did he have in 1971?

10. This player scored 103 points in 1971 and reached 100 points or more for three straight seasons. Who is he?

11. What university did he play for?

12. What was Earl McCullough's nickname?

13. What round was Ken Sanders drafted in during the 1972 draft?

14. How many seasons did he play for Detroit?

15. Name the two top defensive players who retired after the '72 season.

16. What all-time Lions records does each hold?

17. How many TD passes did Landry throw in '72?

18. How many did he rush for that year?

19. What team did Don McCafferty coach to a Super Bowl victory prior to coming to Detroit?

20. What year was that Super Bowl played, and who was McCafferty's opponents in the game?

21. This Lions assistant coach was elected to the Pro Football Hall of Fame in 1973 as an end for the Baltimore Colts. He would go on to coach the New England Patriots to a Super Bowl appearance in 1985. Name him.

22. Name the player who intercepted three passes and returned one 95 yards for a TD against the Chicago Bears on November 18, 1973.

23. Who led the team in tackles in 1973 with 55?

24. Where was Rick Forzano head coach before becoming an assistant with Detroit?

25. What round was Dexter Bussey drafted in '74?

26. What round was Gary Danielson drafted in?

27. What Washington Redskins quarterback did the Lions trade for in '74? (Hint: he later went on to coach the Cincinnati Bengals to a

Super Bowl appearance.)

28. What team did the Lions trade Mel Farr to?

29. What did the Lions receive from this team as compensation, and what player did they get from Cleveland as part of the deal?

30. Who was the Lions' opponent for their final game at Tiger Stadium?

31. What day was the game played on?

32. What was the score of the game?

33. Who led Detroit in rushing yards in 1972, '73 and '74?

34. What round was Doug English selected in during the '75 draft?

35. What was the original name of the Pontiac Silverdome?

36. What is the actual capacity of the Pontiac Silverdome?

37. What was the projected cost of the stadium?

38. What is the name of the Silverdome's dining room?

39. The first game ever played in the dome was a pre-season game on August 23, 1975. Who was the Lions' opponent that day?

40. October 6, 1975 was the date of the Silverdome's first regular season game. Who was the Lions' opponent for the "Monday Night Football" showdown, and what was the final score?

41. What team did Detroit defeat for its first victory in the Pontiac Silverdome on October 12, 1975?

42. Who filled in for injured QBs Landry and Munson throughout the majority of the '75 season?

43. Who was waived during the fifth game of the '76 season?

44. How many seasons had he played in Detroit?

45. Where did he rank on the Lions' all-time scoring list at the time he was waived?

46. How many points did he have during his career with the Lions?

47. Who took over his job in '76 and led the team in scoring for the year?

48. Who led the Lions with seven sacks that year?

49. How many sacks did the Lions give up in '76?

50. Who was the team's MVP for the '76 season?

51. Name the team that offensive lineman Bob Kowalkowski was traded to in '77.

52. How many seasons did he play with the Lions?

53. In a 23-19 win over New Orleans on September 25, 1977, how many yards did Detroit gain on the ground?

54. In a game on December 17, 1977, this Lions player scored on a 98-yard kick return and an 87-yard punt return during a 30-21 defeat to the Vikings. Name him.

55. Who led the team with seven interceptions in '76 and six interceptions in '77?

56. Who led the Lions in rushing in '77 with 521 yards?

57. Charlie Sanders retired before the '78 season, after having played for Detroit for 10 years. How many receptions did he finish with for his career?

58. How many times did Charlie Sanders make the Pro Bowl?

59. How many TD receptions did he have for his career?

60. What was the nickname for the Lions' pass rush in the late '70s and early '80s?

61. Name the original members of this famed group in '78?

62. What was Al Baker's nickname?

63. How many sacks did he have during the '78 season? (It established a franchise record.)

64. During a 15-7 victory over Tampa Bay on September 9, 1978, how many passing yards did the Lions' defense "take away" from the Bucs?

65. How many sacks did the Lions' defense register during the '78 season?

66. How many seasons did Paul Naumoff play for Detroit?

67. What team did Greg Landry get traded to?

68. How many times did David Hill make the Pro Bowl squad?

69. Name the rookie QB who played for an injured Danielson and Reed in '79.

70. How many INTs did he throw for the season?

What college or university did each play for?

71. Charlie Sanders

72. Charlie Weaver

73. Paul Naumoff

74. Greg Landry

75. Steve Owens

7
A Sooner in Lions Clothing
(1980-83)

One good thing about the draft system incorporated by the National Football League is that the bad teams have a golden opportunity to get out of the basement; they get first crack at the galaxy of hot commodities coming out of the college ranks each year. To use an astronomy analogy, we find out later if they turn out to be a comet West or a Kohoutek.

TIME OUT:
Kohoutek was an extremely bright comet when astronomers observed it approaching the inner solar system. Astronomers speculated that it would be "the comet of the century" when it neared the sun, putting on a great naked eye show in 1974. But it failed to live up to expectations, and most of the general population did not have a chance to view it. Three years later, a less-heralded comet West surpassed its promise and dazzled viewers to become one of the best comets of the 20th Century.

TIME IN:
Only the truly bad or unlucky teams flounder for any length of time. A more recent example would be the lowly "Yuccaneers" of the mid-'80s to mid-'90s, a team which never seemed to be able to pull out of the proverbial nose dive, no matter how many high draft choices they received. When they did draft wisely—players like Bo Jackson or Vinny Testeverde—they either turned their backs on them or had trouble dis-

tinguishing teammates from the opposition. Of course, free agency plays a major role in the process now, but back then, the NFL draft was where all of a team's dreams and visions were conceived.

Once in a while, a dominant superstar comes along. Hopefully your team's personnel director can detect one. (An easy jab here would be to say, "What were you guys thinking?" to a certain rival team who passed on Barry Sanders to draft one Mr. Tony Mandarich, but that would be too easy.)

A last place finish in 1979 gave the Lions just that opportunity. Detroit needed somebody to liven things up on the field. It was up to the ownership, the coaching staff, the scouts, and the draft gurus to discern which guy would best jump start the team for its travel down the road to recovery. There were two Heisman Trophy winning running backs up for grabs, and it was known early on that the Lions wanted one of them.

The two coveted running backs were Charles White out of USC, Heisman winner in '79, and Oklahoma's Billy Sims, honoree in '78 as a junior. Players' status often rise and decline during the weeks preceding the draft, and while White's stock fell, Lions' personnel determined Sims to be a sure-fire pick. Detroit chose Billy as the overall number one selection in the 1980 draft. He would provide a bevy of fireworks during his short career.

A funny story about Billy's arrival in the Motor City reveals the type of player the Lions got. Showing up his first day in a banged-up Chevy truck (Sims sure knew how to suck up to his new employer), he was greeted with the usual cold shoulder rookies know so well. Only this man warranted an extra dose. He had signed for a then unbelievable sum of $1.7 million over three years, more than most of the proven veterans were making. And the fanfare attached to his image had invaded the clubhouse long before the arrival of Billy Sims the ballplayer. For all that any of the other players knew, this hotshot could have been a dud. But Billy had pizzazz, and the first shot he had at demonstrating it was during the yearly training camp ritual of meet the rookies.

Sims stood up and said: "I'm Billy Sims from Oklahoma, and I'm the reason you guys didn't get raises this year."

It was obvious Billy was going to fit in. It was made even more obvious the first time he pulled a Detroit Lions jersey over his back and began harassing foes with his footwork. He commanded the respect of his teammates from the get-go, practicing not like a spoiled superstar, but sweating, working, drilling the same way as a guy fighting for his survival with the club.

With Sims, the Lions were a contender again.

Here's a chance to relive some of the memories:

September 7, 1980: Visiting the Super Bowl runner-up LA Rams as heavy underdogs, the Lions play with a new mentality, sparked by the explosiveness of their rookie runner. Billy snares a Gary Danielson pass, cuts the corner, leaving defenders grasping at air and chewing dirt, and totes the ball 60 yards to set up the go-ahead touchdown in the third quarter. A relentless attack shows no mercy on LA, as the Lions rout the Rams, 41-20.

September 28, 1980: A sellout crowd at the Silverdome witnesses the rejuvenated Lions offense destroy the Vikings, 27-7. The Lions are an amazing 4-0 to begin the year.

Throughout the season, Sims eluded would-be tacklers with finesse and bowled over others with his power. The Lions finished 9-7 during Sims's rookie campaign, missing the Playoffs by a tie-breaker scenario to Minnesota, thus alerting the league to beware in the seasons to come. Sims established many team records during the year on his way to becoming the consensus pick for the NFL's top rookie.

November 19, 1981: Arguably the greatest debut ever made by a Detroit Lions player is witnessed on national television, as an unheralded Eric Hipple engineers a 48-17 blitzkrieg of the Chicago Bears on "Monday Night Football". Without Billy Sims, who sits out the game due to a toe injury, the Lions offense invades their arch enemy through the air, raining bombs and direct strikes at will on a befuddled Bears defense. Hipple's aerial superiority that night, including four TDs and 336 yards, is backed by his own personal ground assault, as he rushes for two more scores.

December 20, 1981: A final regular season showdown for the NFC Central division crown turns into a heart-breaking affair for the home town Lions. Detroit enters the game 7-0 at the Silverdome for the season. An up-and-down struggle with the Tampa Bay Bucs keeps fans buzzing throughout the 60-minute battle. On fourth down of Detroit's final drive, Hipple launches a bomb that is knocked away by a Bucs defender, and the Lions' playoff hopes crumble under a 20-17 defeat.

September 19, 1982: After stating that he would get the Lions into the Playoffs this year no matter what, Sims rushes for 119 yards and goes over the century mark for receiving, as Detroit beats the LA Rams, 19-14.

Detroit began the year with two victories, but a 57-day players strike hurt the Lions more than any other NFL team. After the schedule resumed, Detroit lost the first three games, wiping out any momentum they had gained prior to the strike. Fortunately for every team in the league, a substitute playoff format was used for the shortened season. The top eight teams from each conference were placed in a Super Bowl derby. With two wins in the final four weeks of the season, Detroit made the cut as the eighth and final seed in the National Football Conference. Sims backed up his boast by getting his team into the Playoffs, despite a weak 4-5 record.

January 8, 1983: The Lions run into a Washington Redskins football machine that is led by the bulldozing of fullback John Riggins and the precision passing of Joe Theismann. A powerful offensive line, known as "the Hogs", manhandles the Detroit D, while Sims and Company is unable to consistently get the ball into scoring position. Detroit's first playoff appearance since 1970 ends as a 31-7 defeat.

For the Lions though, the pendulum was on the upswing. Once again, the 11th hour would determine the team's playoff fate in 1983. It would go down in the history books as one of their most memorable seasons.

December 18, 1983: Again the season finale in the Silverdome against Tampa Bay is the stage for Detroit's run at the division title. Eric Hipple sprains his left knee in the third quarter of a close game, and it is up to Gary Danielson to come in cold and heat up the offense. He emerges a hero by leading Detroit to their game-winning score in a 23-20 victory.

December 31, 1983: Detroit finds out that football is a game of yards and inches after a classic struggle with the San Francisco 49ers in their divisional playoff game. For the most part, the game is a see-saw battle, with both teams moving the ball. Billy Sims gives Detroit a 23-17 advantage with two minutes left. But Joe Montana rips off large portions of the field in blazing speed and puts San Francisco back on top 24-23. The Lions decline to let the game slip away. Sims, a workhorse throughout the game, manages to position Detroit into field goal range. One of the most memorable moments in Lions history comes when Eddie Murray cocks his leg and boots the potential game winning 43-yard field goal with five seconds remaining. The ball travels through the air, while Monte Clarke raises his hands in prayer along the sidelines. Unfortunately, the ball sneaks inches to the outside of the upright, ending the game, destroying the hopes of a football team ...

A devastating five seconds for a team that had come so far. It was made more devastating after the turn of the upcoming season when the team was hit with a barrage of bad luck and bad play. There would not be a chance to make up for those futile few seconds in San Francisco until another great running back donned a Detroit Lions' jersey more than five years later.

TRIVIA QUESTIONS

1980-1983

1. What team was Monte Clark head coach of before he accepted the post for the Lions?

2. What Lions defensive end announced his retirement before the '80 season to start a job in the oil business?

3. What high school did Billy Sims attend?

4. What did Billy wear under his Lions jersey during games?

5. How many TDs did Sims score in his first game as a Detroit Lion on September 7, 1980 vs. the Rams?

6. How many yards did he rush for in his debut?

7. How many yards rushing did Sims finish his rookie year with?

8. How many TDs did he score?

9. What team was the first to defeat the Lions in the '80 season, by a score of 43-28, on October 5?

10. Who led the team in scoring as a rookie in 1980?

11. How many points did he score?

12. What round was he drafted in?

13. How many yards passing did Gary Danielson have in 1980 to set a then team record for most yards passing in a season?

14. Who began punting for the Lions in 1980 and continued the duties through '82?

15. How many sacks did Al Baker register in '80?

16. Who was the team's #1 pick in the '81 draft?

17. Who caught Eric Hipple's first NFL pass?

18. Who did Hipple replace at QB in '81?

19. Who did the Lions defeat in the '81 season opener by a score of 24-17?

20. On November 15, 1981, Detroit defeated Dallas, 27-24, on a last second 47-yard field goal. What was the controversy on that final play of the game?

21. The Lions set a team record for most rushing attempts in one season during 1981. How many did they have that year?

22. How many yards did Sims rush for that season?

23. How many total TDs did he have in '81?

24. Name the second Lions' receiver to gain over 1,000 yards in a season?

25. Who led the team with 11 sacks in 1981?

26. How many seasons did he play with the Lions?

27. What two offensive categories did the Lions lead the league in during the '81 season?

28. Super Bowl XVI was played in the Silverdome on January 24, 1982. What two teams played in that Super Bowl and what was the outcome?

29. What team did Monte Clark's son Bryan get drafted by as a QB in 1982?

30. What Lions offensive lineman made the pro bowl for the '82 season?

31. What Lions player retired after suffering a neck injury in a game against Minnesota on December 19, 1982?

32. How many rushing yards did Billy Sims gain in the '82 playoff game at RFK Stadium?

33. Name the three players who led the team with six sacks each during the strike shortened '82 season.

34. What USFL team tried to sign Billy Sims for the 1983 season?

35. How much did Ford sign him for over five years to keep him in a

Lions uniform?

36. What Detroit Lion became the first veteran NFL-er to join the USFL?

37. What team had the Lions acquired him from in 1980?

38. What team was Al Baker traded to?

39. What team was guard Russ Bollinger traded to?

40. How many times did Doug English make the Pro Bowl squad?

41. How many rushing attempts did Sims have against Green Bay on November 20, 1983, during a 23-20 overtime win in Milwaukee, setting a then team record?

42. He established a personal best mark for yards rushing in that game. How many did he have?

43. What team did Eddie Murray kick a 54 yard field goal against, equaling a then team record, on December 11, 1983?

44. What major defensive category did Detroit lead the NFC in for '83?

45. Who led the team with 13.5 sacks in '83?

46. Who did Lions teammates name as the one Lion who most represented the concept of good sportsmanship throughout his career with the franchise?

47. What other two honors did fans vote him for during his career?

48. How many times did Billy Sims make the pro bowl?

49. How many times was Sims the Lions' offensive MVP?

50. Who took over punting duties in '83?

51. What team did the previous punter go to that year?

52. How many INTs did Danielson throw in the playoff game at San Francisco on December 31, 1983?

53. What was the Lions' home record in '83?

54. Who led the team with seven INTs that season?

55. Who was Detroit's top kick returner 1981-83?

56. Who led the team in tackles for four straight seasons 1980-83?

What numbers did they wear?

57. Dexter Bussey

58. Doug English

59. Ken Fantetti

60. William Gay

What college or university did each play for?

61. Eric Hipple

62. Doug English

63. Ken Fantetti

64. Al Baker

65. William Gay

66. Freddie Scott

67. Dexter Bussey

68. Gary Danielson

8
The Seven-Year Drought (1984-90)

Perhaps no other team in the NFL is more familiar with feast and famine than the Detroit Lions. Unfortunately, the Lion was beginning to look a little scrawny by the mid-'80s. Their usual prey of Vikings, Packers, and Bears had become adept at eluding the beast. Even the young Buccaneers had been feisty of late. Echoes of their last championship in '57 rung through the roars of Lions fans down the stretch in '83, only to come up short, only to open the flood gates to losing season after losing season.

The seven-year drought that followed the playoff appearance is a phase unequaled in team history. Not even during the miserable '40s was such a chain of sub-par seasons forged and dragged around the ankles of the team, as it seemed. Though disappointing, the fans and the team would learn to bear through it.

"Maybe next year!" became the fans' motto. Their modest hopes kept their eyes to the future where the team had yet to lose one game. It was a way to persevere. Call it optimism of the heart.

Of course, the fans were not the only ones suffering. After all, there is no place to hide from shame on a football field. Athletes hate to lose, and the more they do, the louder the grumbles are from the competitive animal inside.

The worst case scenario hit the team on October 21, 1984, when Billy Sims tore cartilage and two ligaments in his right knee during a contest at Minnesota. Detroit held on to beat the Vikings, 16-14, but Sims career was over. All attempts to rehabilitate the damaged knee were not successful enough to warrant a comeback. So the greatest

Lions runner up to that time officially announced his retirement in 1986. At the end of his career, Billy Sims owned the Lions' rushing record book. Of course, it would be re-written a few years down the road, but the impression made by Billy Sims will last forever.

More dilemmas surfaced during the campaign. Eric Hipple was also a casualty to a bad knee in week three. Gary Danielson stepped back in and performed admirably, but the lack of bite from the ground game hurt the offense to no end. The result was a disastrous 4-11-1 season.

Darryl Rodgers took over as head coach the next year. An impressive six wins at home against the likes of San Francisco, Dallas, and AFC powers Miami and the NY Jets were the highlights. As big as those wins were, they were muted somewhat by road losses to the Colts and the Bucs in OT, as well as a blowout loss to the 8-8 Packers, 43-10. Overall, Rodgers' first year turned out to be a conservative and sometimes boring 7-9 season.

Another debacle happened the following year. Detroit finished in third place. They could thank the "Bay of Pigs", as Chris Berman refers to them, for that lofty position in the standings. The Pack and the Bucs were almost flawlessly pathetic in 1986. While the Lions lost close games that added up to a 5-11 year, Green Bay and Tampa were in a majority of lopsided games that resulted in 4-12 and 2-14 records, respectively. Both teams, however, did manage to defeat Detroit in the Silverdome, the low points of a low season.

Digging deeper into the trench of pro football obscurity, Detroit posted a 4-11 mark in 1987. They joined Tampa in the cellar that year, though its hard to admit even now. If you were to try and fetch up a highlight of the season, a 27-17 victory over the sliding Cowboys (7-9) or Jim Arnold's punting would have to suffice. Former number one draft choice Chuck Long, though he flashed signs of brilliance, was never properly utilized by the coaching staff. Long had the talent, but, just as it would occur in later years, Detroit did not know how to groom a young QB, or teach him through his miscues.

Although the immediate results were unseen, 1988 began a long process of remodeling the club. Maybe the two best moves made by the Darryl Rodgers regime was drafting "Mr. All-Out" Chris Spielman at linebacker and a devastating punisher in Bennie Blades at safety. His other moves were mostly fruitless.

Spielman would automatically inject a new attitude into the defense. Right from the start he proved what type of a player he would be, by showing up early to practice in order to gain any edge possible, by studying game films and imbedding schemes into the roots of his brain. Ah, the kind of player who eats, drinks, sleeps, and breathes football! Starting with his rookie season, Chris would be the perennial leader in tackles on the team until his departure during the '96 off-season. Small by prototypical standards, but gutsy, he charged to wherever the play was unfolding, throwing himself around, battering his own body, pulverizing opponents. Intense is the word for Chris Spielman.

It was a weak offensive unit at best during the season of '88. With a young, up-and-coming line learning the ropes and a fleet of slow, heavy-footed backs, there was nowhere to run and nowhere to hide from resilient defenders. The passing game rarely showed up for games, as evidenced by the fact that some teams' rushing totals outdistanced the Lions' passing totals.

With a record of 2-9 after a 23-20 defeat to the Buccaneers at home on November 13, Darryl Rodgers was handed his walking papers. Through three-plus seasons, Rodgers compiled an 18-40 record. That speaks volumes, but the coming and going of average players during his occupation magnified his inadequacies at running a pro football team.

The days of an impotent offense soon were over.

Wayne Fontes was promoted to head coach on an interim basis for the remainder of the year. The team responded by winning two of the final five games, sending out a message that they wanted Wayne to stay. Shortly after the season ended, Fontes was given the job.

Along with the change in coaching, came the drastic change in offensive philosophy to the "Run 'n' Shoot." It was a scheme that had the reputation for lighting up the scoreboard, but it did very little to assist the defensive unit or allow them much needed rest between possessions. At least the intricate system did not generate many yawns from action hungry spectators. Of course, it helped having the best new weapon in football.

Regardless of signing three days before the regular season began, Barry Sanders managed to awe the home folks during the '89 opener against the Phoenix Cardinals. *Three days!* Nobody gets in that kind of football shape with only three days preparation. Okay, maybe Superman could, but that's stretching it. Enough cannot be said about the talent of Barry Sanders. Just ask any player who has looked foolish trying to corral the compact back. Pick any runner in the history of the game who could most likely make a cut on a tight rope and the consensus selection would be the Lions' superstar.

As strange as it may now sound, credit is due to the Wayne Fontes staff for selecting Barry with the third pick in the '89 draft. Many scouts and organizations considered him too small for the NFL. Some claimed that he might be too fragile for the pounding initiated by the big brutes that roam on the opposite side of the ball. He had, in fact, proven his durability by handling the ball a multitude of times in college and, as he does at the pro level, handing out more punishment than he takes. Simply put, Barry Sanders avoids the hit.

Rodney Peete was also drafted in 1989. Before suffering an injury late in the pre-season, he had won the starting QB job. As the year unfolded, Peete was available for only half of the games, but when he was in, the offense seemed to click. He emerged as a star on the rise during Detroit's first victory of the year. A game in Tampa Bay on October 15 gave Rodney the opportunity to fulfill a fantasy envisioned by every aspiring QB—heck, by every aspiring kid who has ever picked up a football. Under the two-minute offense, he drove the team down field, finding the kinks in the Bucs defense like a seasoned pro. With 23 ticks remaining and the game on the line, Peete executed a five-yard bootleg to the right and scampered into the end zone for the game-tying score. Eddie Murray put the PAT through, and Rodney Peete was an instant hero.

The Lions finished out 1989 by reeling off five wins in a row to end up 7-9. Barry Sanders was an obvious choice for Rookie of the Year, but the most original aspect of this superstar was his unassuming demeanor. He showed this in the finale by sitting out the last portion of a blowout in order to let his backup get some playing time. One more carry could have given him the rushing title, but personal records did not concern him as much as winning. Detroit toppled Atlanta, 31-24, that day.

One of the all-time first round busts joined the team in 1990. A product of the "Run 'n' Shoot" in college, Andre Ware came with a price tag, but he also came with a slew of NCAA passing records under his belt. Everyone knows that the proper tutelage is as important for an NFL QB as talent is. A lengthy pre-season hold out hindered Ware his rookie year, but with Rodney Peete all ready there, it was difficult for Fontes to make a conclusive decision as to who would be the main guy. Reminiscent of the days of Landry and Munson, it continued the long history of QB controversies introduced by Lions coaches.

A young, upstart offense and a maturing defense was not enough that year, as Detroit began the '90s with six wins and 10 losses. If anything, it was a season full of promise, one that gave Lions fans something to get excited about for the new decade, especially with Barry Sanders in the backfield. Detroit seemed to be on the verge of something big.

Maybe next year!

TRIVIA QUESTIONS

1984-90

1. How many yards did Billy Sims gain in his final game against Minnesota on October 21, 1984?

2. How many yards did that give Sims for his career?

3. His total established a team record, at least until Barry became a Lion. Another running back retired after the '84 season, ending his career second on the Lions' all-time rushing list. Name him.

4. How many yards did this running back have for his career?

5. How long was Sims's longest career run from scrimmage?

6. How many rushing TDs did Sims finish his career with?

7. Who led the Lions in rushing for three straight seasons after Sims was lost from the injury?

8. The running back in the previous question set a then team record for receptions in a season in 1984. How many receptions did he have that year?

9. The Lions played San Francisco at home in an '84 season opening rematch of the '83 playoff game. How did the game end?

10. What linebacker was obtained from Dallas in 1984?

11. How many overtime games did Detroit play that season?

12. What passing feat did Gary Danielson accomplish during the '84 season?

13. What two universities did Darryl Rodgers coach at prior to becoming the Lions' head coach?

14. Who was Detroit's first round draft choice in '85?

15. What veteran quarterback did Detroit acquire before that season?

16. From what team was he acquired?

17. What former 1,000-yard rusher was obtained from Philadelphia in '85?

18. Gary Danielson was traded to Cleveland prior to the start of that season. What did the Lions get in exchange for him?

19. Who took over punt returning duties in 1985 and led the team in that category four consecutive seasons?

20. Who led the Lions in receiving in '85?

21. How many season did he play with Detroit?

22. Who was the Lions' starting center throughout most of the '80s?

23. Where did he play college ball?

24. What was Leonard Thompson's nickname?

25. What defensive lineman retired before the 1986 season after suffering a ruptured disk in his neck the previous season?

26. Name the tight end obtained from Tampa Bay in '86?

27. What offensive lineman did the Lions acquire from Houston in 1986?

28. During a 24-21 loss to Cleveland on September 28, 1986, who tied a then team record for most receptions in a game with 12?

29. What team record did Eric Hipple establish during the same game?

30. Who threw a 34-yard TD on his first NFL pass in a game on November 23, 1986?

31. What university did he play at?

32. Who caught the TD?

33. Who were the Lions playing that day?

34. Who led the team with 995 yards receiving in '86?

35. How many receiving TDs did Leonard Thompson finish his career with?

36. Who was Detroit's number two pick in the '87 draft?

37. Due to the NFL's player strike, the third week of the '87 season was canceled. Who were the Lions scheduled to play that day, September 27, 1987?

38. How many of the games in '87 were replacement games?

39. Who was Detroit's replacement starter at QB?

40. What former Lions player punted six times during replacement games?

41. Excluding strike games, Chuck Long played QB the entire season. How many INTs did he throw in '87?

42. Who was the only Lion player who made the Pro Bowl squad for the '87 season?

43. Who was acquired to play QB after the sixth game in '88?

44. What team was he acquired from?

45. Who was the Lions' opponent on November 20, 1988, Wayne Fontes's first game as head coach?

46. Who did Wayne hire as offensive coordinator after becoming head coach?

47. Who was named the team's offensive MVP for the '88 season?

48. What name was given to the Lions' "Run 'n' Shoot" offense?

49. What team was Mel Gray picked up from as a plan B free agent?

50. What round was Rodney Peete drafted in?

51. Who was the Lions' QB when Rodney was injured during the '89 season?

52. Who led the team in receptions in '89 and '90?

53. How many yards receiving did he have in '89?

54. How many receiving yards did he gain during a home game on December 3 of that year against New Orleans?

55. The Lions led the league in rushing TDs in '89. How many did they have?

56. How many rushing TDs did Barry Sanders have during his rookie year?

57. Eddie Murray made the pro bowl for the '89 season. He converted 20 field goals. How many attempts did he have for the year?

58. What running back was acquired from Washington for the '90 season?

59. Who were the Lions second and third round picks in the 1990 draft?

60. In a game on November 4, 1990, in which Washington came from behind to defeat Detroit, 41-38, in OT, how many total yards did the Lions allow?

61. Who led the team in sacks from 1987-90?

What college or university did each play for?

62. Eddie Murray

63. James Jones

64. Michael Cofer

65. Rodney Peete

9
The House That Wayne Built (1991-Present)

He came with the excess baggage of wearing his emotions on his sleeve. There have been more calls for his head than all of Henry VIII's wives heads put together. The chair in his office is a 24-hour hot seat. A player's coach who takes the brunt of the storm (i.e., the numerous potshots delivered by media, critics, and fans alike), Wayne Fontes's Lions have avoided the internal destruction that has appeared on the verge more often than not during his reign. Until Scott Mitchell had a blockbuster season in '95, Wayne had a habit of playing musical QBs that upset offensive production year after year. Assistants have come and gone. From the choices made by his staff, stars have been made, deals have turned into busts. Yet he built a team around a promise to "Restore the Roar," and overcame the blunders and the injuries, the tragedies, all the doubters, and hecklers to preserve a place for his team in the Lions' hall of fame. Love him or hate him, Wayne Fontes has brought a winner to town.

Fontes has been dubbed "the Teflon Coach" for his ability to dodge the firing squad, but a more fitting nickname would be "the Adhesive Coach." Fontes is like glue. His genius lies in holding his team together, no matter what tribulations they encounter.

It did not take him long to ingrain a positive attitude. By 1991, the Lions were fed up with losing.

If a fortune-teller had told Detroit fans and media that the Lions would be contending for a Super Bowl directly following a blowout loss in the season opener, everyone would have rolled their eyes and considered the prediction supernatural baloney. But it was destined to become a season full of tragedy and unsung heroes. Sure, there would be hints of Cinderella going to the ball, but the Lions' season was as indicative of hope and triumph of the human spirit as it was of being a fairy-tale.

Barry Sanders sat out the first game in Washington with sore ribs, and the team was steam rolled by a Redskins juggernaut, 45-0. Already the Lions were being written off. Some said they were the worst team in the league.

Nobody got down on themselves. Fontes made sure of it. Detroit rebounded by winning the next five in a row, including one of the greatest games in the Detroit Lions' modern era. With the team trailing Minnesota, 20-3, late in the fourth quarter, fans began to pour out of the Silverdome. They would have to listen on radio, as the Lions scored three touchdowns in the final six minutes. First came a bomb from Peete to Robert Clark for a TD, then the recovery of an on-side kick, followed by a quick score. Finally, after putting the clamps on the Minnesota offense, Barry took over. He wound and spun his way to the end zone for the final score. Detroit stole a 24-20 victory.

A 35-3 embarrassment to San Francisco proved to be one more climb over adversity, as Fontes and his team again refused to collapse. The future kings of the NFL, the Dallas Cowboys, led by third year QB Troy Aikman and sophomore runner Emmitt Smith, traveled to Detroit to be fed a spoonful of hard knocks. The Lions executed in every aspect of the game, including a blocked field goal for a touchdown, during a 34-10 win.

The win came at a cost, as Rodney Peete ruptured an Achilles tendon that shelved him for the remainder of the year. A virtual unknown—shades of Eric Hipple's debut, where even the die-hard fans had no idea who the heck the new passer was—stepped into the limelight and tossed two perfect TD strikes that day. With Andre Ware still struggling, it was this journeyman who literally held the fate of the team in his throwing hand. His name was Erik Kramer, but he might as well have been called Erik the Great, since he would finish the season by playing some of the smartest quarterback in the team's last 15 years.

The pinnacle of the heart-tugging season was the scene in a silent Silverdome where Mike Utley lay paralyzed after a tragic play in which the base of his head landed hard on the turf. The play had occurred on a go-ahead TD pass against the Rams on November 17. As he was being taken off the field on a stretcher, he miraculously summoned the strength to issue his teammates and fans a courageous "thumbs up."

The Lions won the game that day, and "thumbs up" became their rallying cry, their dedication to play hard and win the rest of the season, as their fallen teammate would have done. Utley was a true warrior on the football field, and he has confronted paralysis with as much vigor. His struggle is ongoing, but his will and optimism is undaunting. When you think of a lion and think of courage, no one fits the description better than Mike Utley.

Detroit did not lose another regular season game in 1991. A 17-14 overtime upset at Buffalo capped off a 12-4 year. It was the most wins in franchise history.

For the first time since 1957, the Lions hosted a playoff game. Jimmy Johnson brought his Cowboys into the Dome bent on stopping Barry Sanders. They did not count on Erik Kramer exploiting their defense at will. He passed for 341 yards and three TDs as Detroit beat Dallas, 38-6. A Hollywood braintrust would have been hard pressed to find a more inspiring story than the 1991 Detroit Lions.

Unfortunately, the great season ended on the same field that it dismally began. Kramer struggled through the championship game at RFK stadium, and Washington capitalized on numerous Lions turnovers. A close game at half-time (17-7) turned into a lopsided 41-10 victory for the Redskins.

It was the closest Detroit has ever been to the Super Bowl.

As glorious as that season turned out to be, 1992 was marred by more tragedy. During the off season, Len Fontes, defensive backs coach and brother to Wayne, died at home from a heart attack on May 8. Offensive guard Eric Andolsek, who, like Utley was becoming a Pro Bowl caliber lineman, was trimming weeds in his yard in Thibodaux, Louisiana, on June 23, when a truck unexpectedly ran off the road, struck him, and killed him. The team played through, but the season had drastically changed from one of promise to one filled with more heartache.

The Lions fell to 5-11. Kramer played third string behind Peete and Ware. I guess some things in football are not meant to be understood.

After struggling through three fourths of the '93 campaign, Fontes's job was on the line. By then the Lions offense had been modified and new co-ordinator Dave Levy told Wayne that Kramer was the man to lead the team.

Kramer took over during the 13th week and did take the team to another division title. A remarkable feat, considering the Lions had lost Barry Sanders to a knee injury during the Thanksgiving Day loss to Chicago. Barry was back for the playoff game and was as superhuman as ever, but Brett Favre and Sterling Sharpe stunned the Lions by hooking up on a devastating final minute TD pass that secured a 28-24 Green Bay victory.

If it had appeared that Detroit was inching closer to becoming an elite team, no one would have noticed it by the coach's actions. Fontes built this house, and now he was cleaning it during the spring of '94. With the three-headed monster of Peete-Ware-Kramer at quarterback having departed, the biggest need was a franchise quarterback. And the Lions were willing to spend big bucks in the free agent market to find one. In this day and age of free agency, you can virtually buy a better team overnight. Unlike grooming a draftee and running the risk of a team's investment not panning out when it comes time to put up, a proven player can pay big dividends. For better or for worse, its just another way that the game has changed. In a highly publicized deal, Wayne Fontes and his staff flew to Miami to visit Scott Mitchell and offered a lucrative contract to Dan Marino's four-year back up. Some called it a ludicrous deal, but Mitchell was considered by others to be the prize catch of the off-season.

Mitchell had made seven starts in '93, resembling little of Dan Marino in technique, but proving he was a legitimate starter of the future. The future arrived in '94. Essentially, he was a little-experienced rookie when he started for Detroit to begin the season. Scott looked impressive in victories over Atlanta and a memorable overtime defeat of the Dallas Cowboys on "Monday Night Football", but the southpaw fought through injuries and inconsistency. He was tabbed a "bust" after he went down for good due to a fractured wrist during the ninth game in Green Bay.

Lucky for the Lions, Fontes had also picked up crafty veteran Dave

Krieg, not only to show the young Mitchell the ropes of his craft, but to provide a $1 million insurance policy. Krieg was worth every dollar. He got in a zone and never came out of it, leading Detroit to five wins in the last seven games. His stats: 16 TDs with a mere three interceptions. The Lions eked out a wild card birth at 9-7.

On the frozen tundra of Lambeau Field, a swarming Packer D, led by Reggie White, pushed back the Detroit offensive line and gang-tackled Barry Sanders. He was held to a remarkable—dare I say it—minus one yard rushing. Green Bay won, 16-12, solidifying their modern day image as the Lions arch rival.

What a mess 1995 started out to be. Yet it would be one more memorable season held at the seams by the indomitable coach. At 0-3, the chants for Wayne Fontes's removal was voiced loudly from the tiers of the Silverdome. But the Lions were giant-killers on "Monday Night Football" as they had proved the year before. They beat another defending Super Bowl champion on Monday night in '95. This time it was the San Francisco 49ers by a score of 27-24. For the game, the offense had been altered to accommodate the talents of receivers Herman Moore, Brett Perriman, and Johnnie Morton. Under the simplified system, Scott Mitchell began to come of age.

A loss to Atlanta, 34-22, dropped Detroit to 3-6, and the chants for Wayne Fontes dismissal grew louder. Fans threw out jeers, Fontes ducked. The media criticized him, he sang "Frosty the Snowman." Owner William Clay Ford issued a Playoffs-or-else ultimatum to his coach, and Fontes responded by performing his greatest escape by reeling off seven straight to close out the regular season. Mitchell matured into one of the top QBs of the year by spreading the ball around to his vast assortment of targets. Lions fans were able to brag about having the best offense in the league. Records fell with regularity. To borrow a *Star Wars* analogy, the Lions offense had more fire power than the Death Star. Detroit became the first team in NFL history to have a 4,000-yard passer (Mitchell), a 1,500-yard receiver (Moore), and a 1,500- yard rusher (Sanders) in one season. Moore and Perriman became the first receiving duo to each snare over 100 receptions in a season, also setting a new NFL yardage mark along the way.

Being the hottest team in the NFL going into the Playoffs, Lomas

Brown predicted an easy victory over Philadelphia in the first round. According to the Pro Bowl offensive linemen, it was not a matter of whether Detroit would win, but by how much. My guess is he meant the Lions, but he would have been prophetic if he had meant the Eagles. Detroit picked a bad time to play their worst game of the year. Perriman suffered a leg injury, Mitchell resembled a rookie for 30 minutes, and the Eagles—fired up by Brown's boast—took advantage of every Lions miscue. A minor comeback late in the game was meaningless, as Detroit stumbled out of Philly with a 58-37 loss.

It appeared that Fontes's job was in jeopardy once again. Ford had watched the playoff debacle from the press box at Veteran's Stadium, convinced he had the better team. Critics believed the team's collapse did not bode well for the coach.

It was thought that as Mitchell went so too did Fontes. After all, it was the coach's biggest gamble. Well, Scott had a Pro Bowl caliber season, and Fontes did rally his team into the Playoffs. Having made the post-season three years in a row, and with an offensive nucleus second to none, Wayne Fontes had built a formidable house in the Pontiac Silverdome. He earned another shot.

But it always seems that Wayne Fontes is one step away from the Super Bowl, or one blunder from joining the unemployment line.

TRIVIA QUESTIONS

1991-Present

1. What university did Fontes play football and baseball at?

2. What position did he earn All-Big Ten honors at for football?

3. What NFL team drafted him in '62?

4. How many seasons did he play for them?

5. What high school did Fontes win a Michigan Class B state

championship with in 1967 as a head coach?

6. What future NFL coach did he serve as defensive backs coach for at USC?

7. What NFL team did he first coach for, first as defensive backs coach, then as defensive co-ordinator, and later assistant coach?

8. What year did he become the Lions' defensive co-ordinator?

9. How many Lions made the '91 Pro Bowl squad?

10. Name them.

11. Who did Fontes name as receivers coach in '91?

12. Name the offensive lineman that was recognized on *USA Today*'s 1991 all-pro team.

13. What university did Mike Utley play football for?

14. What number did he wear as a Lion?

15. What round was Utley drafted in during the '89 Draft?

16. What university did Eric Andolsek play football for?

17. What number did he wear as a Lion?

18. Andolsek's last game was the NFC title game at Washington. Including that game, how many consecutive games had he started at left guard with Detroit?

19. What team was Brett Perriman acquired from in '91?

20. During the '91 season, Mel Gray became the first NFL player to

do what?

21. What was the score of the 1992 Pro Bowl, in which Wayne Fontes was the NFC's head coach?

22. How many Lions made that Pro Bowl squad?

23. Name them.

24. Eddie Murray was waived prior to the '92 season, but stands as the team's all-time leading scorer. How many points did he total during his career with the Lions?

25. Who was voted NFL Offensive Rookie of the Year for 1992?

26. Who was Detroit's defensive MVP in '92?

27. Name the linebacker acquired in a Draft day trade in '93.

28. What was his former team?

29. Who was Detroit's first draft choice in '93?

30. Who played running back for an injured Barry Sanders in '93?

31. After Sanders's backup was injured, who played RB for Detroit through the remainder of the regular season?

32. Name the rookie linebacker who was converted to tight end during that season?

33. Who led the team with 8.5 sacks in '93?

34. How many points did Jason Hanson have in '93?

35. How many Lions made it to the '94 pro bowl squad?

36. Name them.

37. Who attempted the Lions first ever two-point conversion? (It was during a pre-season game against the New York Jets.)

38. Who did Scott Mitchell throw his first NFL TD pass against while playing with Miami in 1993?

39. How tall is Mitchell?

40. What is his full name?

41. What round did Miami draft him in during the 1990 draft?

42. What World League team did he play with in '92?

43. Who did he throw his first regular season TD pass as a Lion against?

44. Who caught the TD?

45. Who is Herman Moore's personal trainer?

46. Who did Moore catch his first NFL pass against in 1991?

47. Who did he catch his first NFL TD pass against?

48. Who won the "Longest Drive" contest at the '95 annual Detroit Lions invitational golf tournament with a 290-yard drive?

49. Who was Detroit's first round draft choice in '95?

50. Jason Hanson broke a long standing record by kicking the longest field goal in club history during a game on October 8, 1995 vs. the Cleveland Browns. How long was the kick?

51. How many receptions did Herman Moore have in '95 to establish a new NFL single season record?

52. How many catches did Brett Perriman have for the season?

53. How many TDs did Mitchell throw during the season to set a new club record?

54. How many yards did he pass for during the season to set a new franchise record?

55. How many TDs did Moore catch during the year?

56. How many points did Hanson score in '95 to set a new club record?

What college or university did each play for?

57. Lomas Brown

58. Chris Spielman

59. Bennie Blades

60. Barry Sanders

61. Herman Moore

62. Jason Hanson

63. Kevin Glover

64. Scott Mitchell

65. Johnnie Morton

10
Championship Games

More so than the regular season, title games are a breeding ground for tradition. After all, nothing invents a pro football team better than championships. Atlanta Falcons tradition goes about as far as Fulton County Stadium and the arm of Steve Bartkowski, but they're young yet by NFL standards. Long-standing teams like the Giants, Bears, and Lions are stuffed with tradition. They have had great teams, and they have won championships.

The Detroit Lions reached the apex during their second year in the NFL—sixth if the Portsmouth years are accounted for. The date was December 15, 1935.

Tod Rockwell of the *Detroit Free Press* summed up the title win best: "At no time during the game did Detroit appear to be other than a champion."

Sleet, rain, and snow made the field of U-D Stadium more suitable for the running game. Only Potsy Clark preferred the element of surprise over a sound strategy to start the game versus the Eastern Division champion New York Giants. Two consecutive 26-yard pass plays caught the Giants' D off guard. After moving the ball to the New York four, Ace Gutowsky sealed the opening drive by plunging into the end zone.

As well as the Lions' offense played that day, their defense was not to be out done. They prevented the Giants from scoring three times in the first half, and they held a good offensive team to seven total points for the game. A Frank Christiansen interception at the Detroit 26 set up the Lions second score of the game, a patented change of direction run for 42 yards by Dutch Clark. Two more running TDs were added in the fourth quarter to give the Lions a 26-7 championship victory. The Lions had demonstrated their prowess with a sharp running attack and out played the Giants in almost every aspect of the game. 15,000 joyous fans in U-D Stadium were in a land of the proud that day.

On December 28, 1952, at Cleveland Municipal Stadium, on a 30-degree afternoon, Detroit looked more like a group of seasoned playoff veterans than the Browns, though Cleveland had been in six previous championships, including the last two NFL title games. (The other four were for the AAC title prior to joining the NFL.) The banged up Browns entered the game without the services of halfback Dub Jones, leading receiver Mac Speedie, and defensive tackle John Kissell.

Bobby Layne scored the only points of the first half on a 2-yard sneak. Doak Walker added a long score in the third quarter to push the lead to 14-0. It was a 67-yard dash that the Browns had believed would be a halfback option, a play that had foiled defenses time and time again. Cloyce Box had drawn double coverage and leveled the two defenders as Walker maneuvered down field.

A Harry Jagade score for Cleveland shaved the lead, but all other efforts were thwarted by a tough Lions defense that tightened up near the goal line. Twice Otto Graham had led the Browns inside the Detroit 10, only to come away empty. A Pat Harder field goal was added to nail a 17-7 victory.

Detroit gave an encore performance in '53. This time it was in front of a home crowd of 54,577, and it was not decided until the final two minutes and eight seconds of regulation.

"It was the toughest game we've ever lost," Cleveland coach Paul Brown commented after the game. "I doubt if any team ever lost a tougher one."

Otto Graham fumbled on his first pass attempt of the game. Les Bingaman pounced on the ball for Detroit at Cleveland's 13. Walker scored from one yard out to give fans delusions of a blowout. But it was a sloppily played game on both ends. Bob Hoernschemeyer turned the ball over at the Detroit six, resulting in Cleveland's first points of the game, a 14-yard kick by Lou Groza. A 10-3 lead at the intermission was wiped out by a nine-yard TD run by Jagade and two more Groza field goals. That make the score, 16-10, in favor of Cleveland.

Layne was left with four minutes and 10 seconds and 80 yards of real estate to contend with. The team worked quickly, airing it out in order to chew up big chunks of yardage. Mostly used at defensive end, Jim Doran became an unlikely hero after he slipped by the secondary and hauled in a 33-yard TD pass from Layne. The play shocked the fans and, more importantly, fooled the Brownies. Doak Walker booted the extra point, and Graham was unable to muster a Layne-like drive of his own. His first pass was intercepted, preserving the 17-16 victory and allowing the celebration to begin.

With the nucleus of the team intact, it was believed that the Lions could become the second team to win the league championship three years in a row. The dream was far from realized. Coach Buddy Parker set a 10:00 p.m. curfew the night before, a custom seldom practiced by Lions players of the time. They knew the importance of the game, and there was no partying that night. Even Layne, known to be the most notorious night hawk of the bunch, complied with the rule. Maybe the team just got too much sleep.

A bad omen occurred early on when Otto Graham slung his first TD pass in three championship outings against Detroit to take a 7-3 lead. It was down hill from then on. All in all, Graham threw three TDs and scored three others himself. Meanwhile, Layne fired six INTs, and the Lions lost three fumbles. Add it all up and the final score was Cleveland 56, Detroit 10.

It would not be the last Cleveland heard from the Lions in the decade. Bobby Layne could only be a cheerleader for the league championship showdown on December 29, 1957. It would be a mirror image of the title game three years back, complete with a reversal of fortune.

Tobin Rote might as well have been a machine that day while pitching four touchdown strikes and adding another one on the ground. Being on the receiving end of the longest TD of the game, Jim Doran was a factor once again. The Lions' D kept Jim Brown at bay most of the afternoon. It was no small order, considering the rookie fullback had been throwing a wrench into defensive schemes all year on his way to amassing the highest ground total in the league. He did score on a 29-yard gallop in the second quarter but was limited to only 69 yards for the game.

It was a lightning quick offense that took the field for the Lions that day. By the time the first 15 minutes expired, Detroit owned a 17-point lead. They upped it to 31-7 by half-time and rolled to 59-14 win. The sellout crowd poured down a standing ovation for Tobin Rote as he exited late in the game. Afterwards, ecstatic fans took to the playing surface to celebrate.

It was a scene Lions fans would love to take part in again.

TRIVIA QUESTIONS

December 15, 1935 (versus the New York Giants)

1. What part of the Lions' game did coach Potsy Clark consider their main weakness going into the battle?

2. How many offensive plays did it take Detroit to score on the opening drive?

3. How many of the Lions played in the first quarter of the game?

4. What future Lions coach intercepted a pass in the fourth quarter and later scored the final TD of the game?

5. Who led the team in rushing during the game?

6. What was the name of the trophy the Lions were awarded for their triumph?

7. How much money did each player receive for the win?

8. Why did Potsy Clark award an extra $55 to Harry Ebding, Butch Morse, and Sam Knox?

9. What did the Lions do with the championship game ball after their victory?

Detroit Lions Facts & Trivia™ 121

December 28, 1952 (at Cleveland)
10. Who was favored in the game and by how many points?

11. The Lions had only two players on their roster with prior championship experience. Name them.

12. What two years did they play in the championship with the Chicago Cardinals?

13. What Lion player recovered the botched punt return by Cleveland's Ken Carpenter in the fourth quarter?

14. Why was a Browns last ditch effort TD nullified by the officials?

15. How many yards did Doak Walker finish the day with?

16. How many passing yards did the Lions finish with?

December 27, 1953 (versus Cleveland)
17. Who was favored in the game and by how many points?

18. Who caused the fumble on Graham's first passing attempt?

19. How many plays into the game did the Lions score their first TD?

20. Who intercepted Graham's final pass of the game to seal the victory?

21. How many receiving yards did Doran have during the game?

22. How many passing yards did the Lions' D hold Cleveland to?

23. How many field goals did Doak miss during the game and how long were they?

24. How many completions did the legendary Otto Graham have during the game?

December 26, 1954 (at Cleveland)
25. What Cleveland player confirmed rumors that he would be retiring after the game?

26. Who intercepted a Graham pass during Cleveland's first drive of the game?

27. Who scored the Lions only TD?

28. Who replaced Layne at QB for the third quarter?

December 29, 1957 (versus Cleveland)
29. What player scored on a 19-yard interception return?

30. What former Lions running back scored for Cleveland in the third quarter?

31. Who passed the final TD for the Lions, and who caught the ball?

32. How long were each of Rote's four TD passes?

33. What player caught two of Rote's TD throws?

34. How many passing yards did Rote have in the game?

35. What did Cleveland coach Paul Brown say the turning point of the game was?

II
The Thanksgiving Day Tradition

Nothing captures pure Americana better than the family come together on Thanksgiving Day; relatives and friends gathered before a feast of turkey, mashed potatoes, cranberry sauce, and pumpkin pie, offering prayers in thanks for the blessings bestowed upon them and—let us not forget—watching football.

Plymouth and Detroit. Places of origin synonymous with the holiday. The first being the colony where Pilgrims and Native Americans broke bread in 1621 to celebrate the plentiful harvest they had grown together; the other a city, a dinner table if you will, that serves up a generous helping of professional football. Memorable games for the most part that have enriched the Lions' history.

Who can forget the Lions scoring 52 points against the Packers in 1951, or a hungry Lions defense gobbling up Bart Starr 10 times (plus one more sack against the backup) in 1962? How about the five interceptions during a 45-3 rout of the Pittsburgh Steelers in 1983, or Walter Stanley's 85-yard punt return in the last minute to steal a 44-40 win for Green Bay in 1986? Or the heart-filled message to Mike Utley prior to a 16-6 victory over the Chicago Bears in '91? O.J. Simpson's 273 rushing yards in 1976? Bobby Layne hooking up with Cloyce Box for a 97-yard score in '53?

The Lions have dominated some of these games, have played the spoiler, and hung tough when they were over matched. Once in a while, the team would be, well, for lack of a better term, a turkey. If anything, the yearly contest is a popular exhibit of the club on a national level.

Today the game can be seen by over 80,000 stadium spectators and an audience of millions across the country. On November 29, 1934, the date of the series' inception, the event was witnessed by a capacity crowd of 26,000 and broadcasted on 94 radio stations nationwide. One of the stations happened to be Detroit's WJR, which was owned by George Richards, president of the Lions football team. It was Richards's idea to have his team play on the holiday, and he convinced George Halas, owner and coach of the Chicago Bears, to come to Detroit and take on the Lions. Chicago played in the first five meetings until the series was suspended in 1939 due to World War II. After being resumed in 1945, the Bears were no longer the annual opponent. Since then, there has been a mix of opponents, with the longest continuing rivalry having been the Green Bay Packers starting in 1951 and lasting for 13 seasons.

Although the Dallas Cowboys have since joined in on the tradition, the Lions are the successful originators. Football is as much a part of the holiday in Detroit as the Thanksgiving Day parade.

TRIVIA QUESTIONS

Turkey Day
1. Who did the play-by-play and color commentary on radio for the first Thanksgiving game against Chicago in 1934?

2. How many games in the series were played at the University of Detroit Stadium?

3. Who was the Lions' opponent for the 1945 game that resumed the series after WWII?

4. The 1946 game drew the smallest crowd ever for the series with 13,010 fans. Who did the Lions play that day?

5. What Lion running back ran for 198 yards against the New York Yanks in the 1950 game?

6. Name the player who ran back two punts for touchdowns against Green Bay in 1951, one for 89 yards and the other for 72.

7. To date, the Lions longest winning streak in the series is six games. Over what six seasons did the streak occur?

8. How many yards did Bart Starr lose from sacks in the 1962 game?

9. Who scored on a Starr fumble in that game?

10. The 1963 contest against Green Bay ended a run of 13 straight games in which the Lions and Packers battled on the holiday. They would not play each other on Thanksgiving again until 1984. What was the outcome of the '63 game?

11. What name has been given to the 1968 game in which the Philadelphia Eagles beat Detroit, 12-0?

12. What year did the Lions score 52 points, the highest total for Detroit in the series?

13. Who did the Lions defeat in the 1970 game by a score of 28-14?

14. In that game, the opposing QB was George Blanda. How old was he then?

15. Who was the Lions' opponent in the 1975 game, the first Thanksgiving game played in the Silverdome?

16. Who sacked Denver QB Craig Morton four times during a 17-14 Lions win in 1978?

17. How many times have the Lions shutout their opponents in the series?

18. Who returned a kickoff 95 yards for a TD to start the overtime period in the 1980 game, giving Chicago a 23-17 victory?

19. Who caught three TD passes during a 31-20 win over the New

York Jets in '85?

20. Who did the Lions defeat 13-10 on Barry Sanders's Thanksgiving Day debut in '89?

21. What milestone did Barry reach during the 24-21 loss to Houston in '92?

22. How many yards did Dave Krieg throw for during the 35-14 rout of Buffalo in 1994?

23. Scott Mitchell established a new franchise record for passing yards in a single game during the '95 victory over Minnesota. How many yards did he throw for in the game?

24. The first quarter touchdown by the Lions in that game was the first points Minnesota had ever allowed on Thanksgiving against Detroit. Who scored on the play?

25. How many times have the Lions been shutout in the series?

PROFILES

Lou Creekmur

TACKLE – LIONS

Gene Gedman

BACK – LIONS

1
Dutch Clark

Despite having 20/100 vision in his right eye and 20/200 in his left, Dutch Clark had the ability to avoid crushing blows and the savvy to be a force at safety. Nobody matched him when it came to pure instinct on the football field. Think of a boxer weaving and slipping punches. That's how Clark was while dodging arms and bodies with the ball securely in his hands. He lacked blazing speed, but he had great control of his movements, which allowed him to get into position to make a play. Field generalship was his specialty, as reflected by coach Potsy Clark's complete trust in Dutch's creativity during games, which included the unveiling of new plays he devised with rookies during practices. Throughout his career, Clark played the single wing tailback slot (a.k.a. left halfback), but because he was the designated signal-caller in Potsy's scheme and threw passes, he was considered a quarterback.

One of Dutch's specialties was the drop-kick. The game then featured a bigger, rounder ball than the version nowadays and was more suited to that style of kicking. He could convert accurately from 40 yards, though field goals were not often attempted. Five or less was the norm per team, per season. Besides, the ball's design was frequently being altered. Drop-kicking soon was a lost art.

While playing for Detroit, Dutch was guaranteed the head coaching job by owner George Richards. It was only a matter of time, dependent upon when Potsy Clark became serious about quitting. It was the main reason for Dutch remaining with the team while he coped with homesickness. He had been born, grown up, and attended college in Colorado where he lived with his wife Dorothy when he wasn't playing football.

After playing-coaching Detroit for two years, he moved his football career to Cleveland. It ended his playing days. Since he was under contract to play with Detroit, Richards wanted to trade him to Cleveland for Johnny Drake. Clark wanted to be coach of the Rams but didn't want to give up any of his future players in exchange for himself. He figured his playing career was winding down anyway, especially since suffering an injured ankle that had limited his playing time during his final season at Detroit. So he cut his ties with Richards, stopped coaching the Lions, and quit carrying the ball all at once. He held the Rams head coaching job for four years before joining the army during World War II.

In later years, he was athletic director at the University of Detroit. Then, after his wife died in 1952, he worked as a tool salesman for a company in Detroit. He died August 5, 1978, in Cañon City, Colorado.

TRIVIA QUESTIONS

1. Where was Clark born?

2. What was Clark's middle name?

3. What number did Dutch wear with the Lions?

4. How many consecutive games did Dutch score a TD in during his college football career?

5. How many years did Dutch lead the NFL in scoring?

6. What was Clark's coaching record with the Cleveland Rams?

7. How many field goals did he kick during his career?

8. How many times was he an all-pro?

9. How many career points did Dutch score?

10. When was he inducted into the College Football Hall of Fame?

2
Bobby Layne

Bobby Layne once said: "I sleep fast and wake up movin'." Sometimes it was not until after 2 a.m. that Bobby Layne would check into bed the night before a game. Call it a reckless practice if you want, but he never suffered from it. According to Layne himself, his sleeping for five or six hours the eve of football allowed him less time to go over the game in his head, a sort of defiance of psychological exhaustion.

It was a life that transcended the football field. Layne has reached the status of an icon, the same that, say, James Dean has become more than just a persona on the silver screen. Think of Detroit Lions football —think of pro football in the '50s—and those who are old enough to remember think of Bobby Layne.

Here are the numbers of a Hall of Fame career: 15 seasons and 175 games; 1,814 completions in 3,700 attempts (49 pct.) for 26,768 yards; 196 TD passes; 2,451 rushing yards plus 25 touchdowns; 34 field goals and 120 PATs out of 124 attempts.

The numbers don't tell half the story.

His accomplishments on the field are often overlooked or underappreciated, but the bottom line is he led Detroit to four championship games in seven years, winning two and being injured along the way to another one. Most of his marks still stand. Even the ones that have been or will be broken, do not matter as much as what he brought to the club —the sheer intensity to just "win, baby, win." Records may well fall, but victories stand the test of time.

To touch on his competitive nature, Layne once said: "I don't care if we're just playing showdown for a nickel a hand, I want to beat your brains in."

It was this will to beat his opponents that charged and re-charged his playing career, as if his attitude ran on a pack of Duracells. Though never pretty on a pitching mound, Layne compiled win after win after win during his college days at the University of Texas. For a while, he even flirted with the notion of playing pro ball when he was offered a minor league contract, but the long hours and monotonous travel involved in pursuing a baseball career did not mesh as well with his personality as football did. There was no doubt in the minds of anybody who played with or against Layne that he could have made it to the Big Leagues.

The Longhorns, guided by two Layne TD passes, won the Southwest Conference football championship in 1945, 12-7, over friend and high school teammate Doak Walker's SMU Mustangs. The following year, he led Texas to a 40-27 Cotton Bowl victory over Missouri. He was voted to several All-American teams in 1946, recognition that led to his being drafted by the Pittsburgh Steelers. Ironically, Pittsburgh was the team he ended his pro playing career with after an injury plagued season in '62.

One of Layne's most legendary off the field escapades came during a court hearing on a drunk driving charge during his heyday in Detroit. Layne and teammate Tom Tracy had stopped at a pizza place one night only to find it closed. Earlier in the evening, they had visited the Sax Club, a bar owned by fellow Lion Les Bingaman. As they drove away from the pizza place, down a well lit avenue, Bobby forgot to turn his car lights on. They were pulled over and a police officer, who said Layne was talking funny and slurring his words, issued him a citation for driving while intoxicated. Instead of avoiding the headlines by paying off the fine, Bobby fought the charge. A good portion of his team showed up at the court hearing and watched their leader and his attorney prove to the judge that his Texas drawl was the reason for the officer's suspicion that he was drunk. Upon his acquittal, the players roared and cheered the way fans of a celebrity would. Even though Layne was cleared of the charge, the incident has outgrown its truths and become a big part of his bad boy legend.

Bobby married Carol Ann Krueger on August 17, 1947. It was a marriage that lasted the rest of his life, testimony that there was much more to Bobby Layne than the playboy image sewn directly to his reputation. They had two sons, Rob and Alan. Both boys played collegiate football.

His competitiveness and lifestyle aside, Layne was a compassionate man. He often provided people with tickets to Lions games. During his many nights on the town, if Bobby noticed someone was depressed or not having a good time, he'd shoot a game of pool with them, buy them a drink, or slip them some extra cash. Even total strangers. He liked to make sure others were having as good a time as he was. He was often known to cover the tabs he and his friends and teammates racked up. Layne did not do it to showoff. He could simply afford the expenses better than they. He was also a practitioner of over-tipping.

In life, Layne survived the beatings dished out by defensive lineman on a weekly basis and three head-on automobile collisions. He had become blind in one eye after a cataract operation. He also underwent two throat operations due to cancer, and his "funny" Texas accent had become coarse. With such a competitive spirit, Layne seemed destined to beat even the grim reaper. But two days after undergoing surgery to stop hemorrhaging in his lower esophagus, Bobby Layne passed away. It was December 1, 1986, a cold day for the people whose lives were touched by Layne made warmer only from the memories he left behind. They celebrated the remembrance of his life, just as he would have wanted it.

You could bet there was one heckuva a party in heaven that same night.

"If I had been to all the places and done all the things I'm supposed to have done, I'd have to be Superman."
—Bobby Layne on the Bobby Layne legend

TRIVIA QUESTIONS

1. Where was Bobby born?

2. What was his middle name?

3. What future teammate did Layne join the merchant marines with?

4. What was his career pitching record with the University of Texas?

5. How many passes did he complete and on how many attempts in the '46 Cotton Bowl victory?

6. Why did Layne refuse to play with the Steelers after they drafted him?

7. During his rookie year with the Bears, Layne was not prone to the hazing system incorporated by veterans. What Bears player was he a "personal slave" to that year?

8. Name the two QBs who started ahead of Bobby in Chicago.

9. Along with a #1 draft pick, how much did the NY Bulldogs pay George Halas and the Bears for the rights to Layne in 1949?

10. What did 350-pound lineman Les Bingaman call Layne upon his arrival in Detroit in 1950?

11. What national magazine featured Bobby on its cover following the Lions championships in '52 and '53?

12. Bobby later recalled how badly the veterans treated the rookie players in training camp, a procedure widely installed throughout the NFL at the time, known as hazing. According to Layne, who received the worst treatment of any rookies during his career with Detroit?

13. How long was Layne's longest career pass play?

14. Of all the rookies on the Lions' squad in 1953, why did Bobby befriend Harry Sewell?

15. What year did Layne lead the league in scoring with 99 points?

16. Name the legendary football coach-owner who said this of Layne: "If I wanted a quarterback to handle my team in the final two minutes, I'd have to send for Layne."

17. How many TDs did Bobby throw during his career with the Lions?

18. How many passing yards?

19. How many rushing TDs did he have during his Lions career?

20. How many times did he represent the Lions in the Pro Bowl?

21. What years were they?

22. How many times was he the Lions' MVP?

23. Who was the Lions' opponent for Bobby Layne's last game with Detroit?

24. What coaching position did he have with Pittsburgh after his playing career ended?

25. What team did he serve as a scout for in '66 and '67?

26. How many INTs did he throw during his career?

27. What year was he inducted into the Michigan Sports Hall of Fame?

28. What year did the Lions retire his number?

29. What is the title of Bob St. John's biography on Bobby Layne?

30. Whose Hall of Fame induction did Layne speak at?

JACK CHRISTIANSEN
HALFBACK   DETROIT LIONS

GENE CRONIN
DEF. END   DETROIT LIONS

HARLEY SEWELL
GUARD   DETROIT LIONS

DAVE MIDDLETON
END   DETROIT LIONS

3
Joe Schmidt

Joe Schmidt on the football field was like a blue (and silver) shark in bloody water. It was only a matter of moments before he nabbed his prey.

Ball carriers around the NFL hated the sight of Joe Scmidt tearing after them. They hated the sound of their own bodies being crunched under a devastating blow. Before Dick Butkus, Mr. Schmidt was the one who handed out punishment in the middle of a football field. Make that every *square inch* of a football field. He wasn't glamorous, nor did he dish out cheap shots to earn the reputation of an intimidator.

Although it appeared to most that he had built-in sonar under his jersey that directed him to the point of the ball, it was through hard work and an undying passion for the game that Joe developed into "the best linebacker in the league," according to Packer legend Paul Hornung. He entered the NFL in 1953, after an injury-riddled career at the University of Pittsburgh. He made the most of his playing time in college, including a game breaking 60-yard interception return for a touchdown during a 22-19 victory over Notre Dame his senior year. Still, he was not considered a sure thing in the NFL. For instance, at 6 feet tall, 218 pounds, many scouts believed he was undersized for his position. If he lacked size or physical ability, he made up for it with a magnetic intensity and a fifth speed on the field, that extra burst that shows up on game day, not on stop watches during 40-yard dash times. Or, as his former coach Buddy Parker put it: "He had an instinct for defense that few players ever acquire."

It was not until mid-season of his rookie year that Schmidt was able to prove himself to the Lions, after starter LaVern Torgeson was knocked out of a game due to injury. He was an immovable rock in the heart of the defense from then on. Schmidt rarely committed errors. Joe missing a tackle was about as possible as Lucy finally letting Charlie Brown kick the ball.

It was a career that spanned 13 playing seasons, one as an assistant coach, and six more years as head coach. Like Bobby Layne, his name is one of the first mentioned when it comes to Detroit Lions football. Also like Layne, he was a leader. He was the defensive signal-caller, the motivator. But he did not escape the battle zone unscarred. Banged up shoulders aided in his decision to call it quits after 1965. The next year was spent as linebackers coach. Just shy of turning 35, Schmidt was elevated to head coach, where he molded a tough defense and brought in enough offensive talent to keep the team a consistent contender for years.

Joe left the working part of the game behind in 1973 to be with his family. After 20 years of giving everything of himself to one team, it was time to enjoy the game from a stadium seat's point of view. Today, he still remains a seminal figure in Lions history.

TRIVIA QUESTIONS

1. What is Joe Schmidt's middle name?

2. What is the name of the high school where he played football?

3. What position did play in high school?

4. What NFL team did Joe's brother John play with in 1940?

5. What round was he drafted in by Detroit during the '53 draft?

6. Schmidt set a Lions record for most fumble recoveries by one player in a single season in 1955. How many did he recover that year?

7. How many games did he play during his career with the Lions?

8. What year was he chosen as the Associated Press NFL MVP?

9. How many years was he the captain of the team?

10. How many years was he selected to the Pro Bowl?

11. How many years was he voted team MVP?

12. How many passes did Schmidt intercept during his career?

13. How many TDs did he score?

14. How many wins did he register as head coach?

15. How many losses?

BARRY SANDERS takes a handoff from SCOTT MITCHELL against the Green Bay Packers.

4
Barry Sanders

Fans of the Dallas Cowboys worship the turf that Emmitt Smith runs on, but fans of the Detroit Lions worship the turf that Barry Sanders cuts, spins, jukes, and fakes defenders out on. There, that once and for all settles the dispute on who the best running back is.

Though another argument in #20's favor can be added: throughout most of Sanders's career, he has not blessed with Troy Aikman, Michael Irvin, Jay Novacek, and a brutish offensive line that blows holes through defenses large enough to drive a tank through. Barry has constantly had to pick his way around, over, and through bodies that penetrate the backfield as soon as he touches the ball. Regardless, Barry is the first to appreciate his line for their efforts, handing out Rolexes after his yearly thousand-plus and paying them compliments in the media. Sanders does the most work on a football field since the days of Earl Campbell and Walter Payton. Payton in fact paid the highest compliment to Sanders during his rookie season when he said: "I don't know if I was ever that good."

He has made more unbelievable escapes than David Copperfield.

One defender from the New Orleans Saints was so amazed when he whiffed on Barry that he swore up and down on the sideline after the play that the Lions running back had split in two at the very moment of his attack. The first time he ever went up against Minnesota, Vikings coach Jerry Burns and his team insisted the officials inspect Sanders to see if his jersey had been sprayed with a silicon substance that would make it slippery. The only thing slippery was Barry's moves. Cornelius Bennett found that out when he thought he had Barry wrapped up as he tossed the back to the turf in the season finale at Buffalo in '91, but Sanders put a hand to the ground for balance and spun away.

People have often called him the human pinball machine, in tribute to the way he bounces off would-be tacklers and racks up the points year to year. His powerful legs and upper body enable him to be a bully when he needs to be. Hard-hitting Joey Browner found that out during a game in the early '90s. Browner, a former Vikings safety, had planted himself, and before he could spring forward to unleash a hit, Barry collided with him and knocked him over, then sprinted for a big gain. In one game, the Chicago Bears defensive line had him wrapped up, but the next thing they knew Barry burst out of the pile and scampered down the sideline for a 40-yard touchdown.

Here's one analogy that fits Barry to a tee. Remember the scene in the second *Rocky* movie when Balboa's trainer, Mickey, instructs him to chase after a chicken until he catches it? To do that, a guy needs to maneuver his body in some uncommon positions. He has to be able to change direction at a split-second's notice, be able to accelerate, stop, then go again. In short, he would look like a fool trying to grasp the fowl. That's a lot like trying to tackle Barry Sanders.

About the only knock on Sanders is that he does not handle the ball all the time near the goal line. Actually, his durability has benefited from not being susceptible to goal line poundings. He maintains fresh legs throughout entire seasons.

It was a fluke that Barry fumbled twice in the final six minutes of a 1995 loss to the Arizona Cardinals. One of his key attributes is that he does not turn the ball over. Prior to those two fumbles, Barry had carried the ball over 800 times without a single turnover.

Born on July 16, 1968 in Wichita Kansas, his father taught him to be humble. Such humility is apparent every time he reaches the end zone and simply flips the ball to an official. Though his coaches thought he was too small, he was converted from defensive back to running back for the final five games of his senior year in high school. It was obvious the coaches knew what they were doing all season, because it took Barry the whole *five* games to break over a thousand yards. It was not until his junior year at Oklahoma State that he was cast into the national spotlight. He began his Heisman Trophy winning year by returning the season opening kickoff for a touchdown.

His 2,628 yards rushing and 39 TDs established NCAA records and cemented the Heisman, though Barry felt the award was as much the team's as it was his alone. In honor of them, he accepted the trophy on national television with his offensive linemen surrounding him.

The Lions never had a more potent weapon. He is the only player in football that warrants eight man fronts to stop him. He hit the 10,000-yard mark for his career in his seventh NFL season. Twice he's won the rushing title, earning Rookie of the Year in '89 and the 1994 Offensive Player of the Year award. He owns virtually every Detroit Lions rushing record while steadily moving up on all-time NFL lists.

10 years from now, he'll be remembered as the greatest Lions player ever.

TRIVIA QUESTIONS

1. Name Barry's high school in Wichita.

2. What is Barry's height?

3. What university did he want to play for prior to his selecting Oklahoma State?

4. Who did Barry play behind as a running back at Oklahoma State his freshman and sophomore seasons?

5. Whose single season NCAA rushing mark did Sanders break in '88?

6. What was Barry's rushing average per carry his junior year at Oklahoma State?

7. His 295.5 all-purpose yards average shattered the old record of 246.3 total yards per game. Whose record did Barry break?

8. Who was the runner-up to Barry in the '88 Heisman voting, and

the player Sanders told reporters he hoped would win it?

9. How many years was Sanders's original NFL contract for?

10. What was the overall dollar amount for that contract?

11. How long was his first ever NFL run during a game against the Phoenix Cardinals on September 10, 1989?

12. How many yards did he gain in his debut?

13. What team was victim to his first ever 100-yard rushing game on September 24, 1989?

14. How many kickoffs did Barry return during his rookie season?

15. For how many yards?

16. What was his rookie season rushing total?

17. How many rushing TDs did he score in '89?

18. Name the quarterback who threw Sanders his first ever TD pass during a 34-27 victory at Minnesota on October 7, 1990.

19. Barry led the league in rushing in 1990. How many yards on the ground did he have that year?

20. What scoring feat did he accomplish in 1991?

21. What team was Detroit playing when he became the Lions all-time leading rusher?

22. What was the date of that game (month and year)?

23. What team did he attempt his first ever NFL pass against on

November 26, 1993?

24. How many yards did he rush for in '93, despite missing the last five games because of a knee injury?

25. How many yards did he rush for in his return against Green Bay in the playoff game that season?

26. Barry holds the Lions' single game rushing record. How many yards did he total for the game to set the record?

27. What team was it against?

28. He also established a franchise record for most rushing attempts in a single game during a classic 20-17 overtime victory over the Dallas Cowboys on "Monday Night Football" on September 19, 1994. How many carries did he have in that game?

29. How many yards did he rush for during the game?

30. What is Sanders' longest career run to date?

31. He made an 84-yard run against Chicago at home on October 23, 1994. What record did the run establish?

32. How many times in '94 was he selected as NFC Offensive Player of the Week?

33. For his 1994 accomplishments, Barry won an "Espy," an ESPN sports award. What "Espy" did he win?

34. Name the late night talk show Barry appeared on in January of '95?

35. Before the two fumbles against Arizona in the third game of the '95 season, what team was the last to recover a Sanders' turnover?

YALE LARY
DEF. BACK — DETROIT LIONS

BILL GLASS
CENTER — DETROIT LIONS

JIM DAVID
DEF. BACK — DETROIT LIONS

TOBIN ROTE
QUARTERBACK — DETROIT LIONS

GENERAL FACTS & TRIVIA

1
The Hall of Fame

Canton, Ohio, is the home to 12 Detroit Lions legends, along with other pro football immortals. The charter year of the Pro Football Hall of Fame was 1963. The Lions were represented by Dutch Clark's election into Canton that inaugural year. Only the greats of the game are enshrined, and as of 1996, there are notable omissions when considering the all-time best Lions. Many fans are surprised to find out that Alex Karras is not a member, or Charlie Sanders, but the obvious have been inducted. An incredible stat: seven of the members played for Detroit during the dominant '50s. Who knows how many future players from Detroit will invent themselves and earn the credentials. But for now, here is a look at the dynamite dozen, in order of induction with their years as a Lion in parenthesis.

DUTCH CLARK (1934-38). One of the original 17 members enshrined.

BILL DUDLEY (1947-49). Played for the Pittsburgh Steelers in 1942 and 1945-46 after World War II, then with the Washington Redskins in 1950, 1951 and 1953. Throughout his career he amassed 8,147 yards rushing, receiving, and returning. He caught seven TDs with Detroit in '47 and was an all-purpose threat with the Lions, including passing. Inducted in 1966.

BOBBY LAYNE (1950-1958). Along with Chuck Bednarik of the Philadelphia Eagles, was the first player elected exactly after the minimum five-year period after his retirement. Inducted in 1967.

ALEX WOJCIECHOWICZ (1936-1948). Played the rest of his career from 1946-1950 as a Philadelphia Eagle. Officials and radio personalities hated to pronounce his name, but he was one of the NFL's legitimate "iron men." He was a powerful blocker and a solid run stopper. He is remembered for his extra wide stance over the ball at center during his Lion career. Inducted in 1968.

JACK CHRISTIANSEN (1951-1958). As a defensive back, Christiansen swiped 46 passes during his career. As a punt returner, he scored eight times. In other words, opposing teams tried their darndest to keep the ball away from him. He was drafted in the sixth round out of Colorado A&M. Detroit got a bargain, huh? Inducted in 1970.

JOE SCHMIDT (1953-1965). Inducted in 1973.

DICK "NIGHT TRAIN" LANE (1960-1965). Finished his career with 68 interceptions. Played with the Los Angeles Rams and the Chicago Cardinals prior to Detroit. He made six Pro Bowls and was an all-pro honoree five times (four as a Lion). His gambling style of play at cornerback made QBs look foolish or even inexperienced. Inducted in 1974.

YALE LARY (1952-53, 1956-64). Besides his outstanding play at safety for 11 seasons, Lary was one of the greatest punters in NFL history. He finished his career with 50 INTs, a 44.3 average on 503 punts. He also had 787 career punt return yards. Inducted in 1979.

DOAK WALKER (1950-1955). Won NFL scoring titles in '50 and '54, totaling 534 points during his career. Though he was not fed the ball a lot, he was one of the league's best runners and a receiving threat. Along with kicking field goals and PATs, he ran back kickoffs and returned punts. Mr. Everything. Doak's #37 was retired on December 11, 1955, his final game at the prime of his career. Inducted in 1986.

JOHN HENRY JOHNSON (1957-1959). For 13 seasons, he was a workhorse running and blocking in the NFL. Johnson's career stats: 6,803 yards rushing and 48 TDs; 156 receptions for 1,478 yards and seven TDs. He played with San Francisco prior to coming to Detroit, then with Pittsburgh, where he topped the hallowed 1,000-yard mark twice ('62 and '64). Inducted in 1987.

LEM BARNEY (1967-1977). Like "Night Train" Lane, whose position Barney played and proved to be no slouch either, opposing teams found out by trial-and-error not to give Lem a chance to get his hands on the ball. His 1,051 return yards on 56 career INTs is a Lions record. He was one of the best kick and punt returners in the game. He made the Pro Bowl seven times. Inducted in 1992.

LOU CREEKMUR (1950-1959). He protected Bobby Layne and led the way for Bob Hoernschemeyer, Walker, Johnson and Co., as if his life—or the team's life—depended on it. One of the Lions' all-time great unsung heroes, Creekmur played in eight consecutive Pro Bowls in 1951-58. Inducted in 1996.

TRIVIA QUESTIONS

1. Along with these 12, there are three other players in the Hall of Fame who spent one season each with Detroit. Name them.

2. What years did each of them play with Detroit?

3. What number did Bill Dudley wear as a Lion?

4. What number did Alex Wojciechowicz wear with Detroit?

5. How many Pro Bowl games did Christiansen play in?

6. How many punt returns for TDs did he have his rookie year?

7. Whose hit record did Dick Lane get his nickname "Night Train" from?

8. How many INTs did Lane nab his rookie year with LA in '52?

9. What number did "Night Train" wear with the Lions?

10. What Washington player did Lane hit in 1953, breaking his opponent's collar bone, thus warranting his nickname to be used in the newspapers for the first time?

11. What is Yale Lary's first name?

12. How many punts did he have blocked during his career?

13. Where did he play collegiate ball?

14. What years did Lary win NFL punting titles?

15. How many pro bowls did he play in?

16. What is Doak Walker's full name?

17. How many pro bowls did he play in?

18. What was John Henry Johnson's nickname?

19. This inductee was the first junior to win the Heisman trophy. Who is he?

20. Where did Lem Barney play collegiate ball?

21. How many career INT returns for TDs did Barney have?

22. What NFL team originally drafted Lou Creekmur?

23. What number did Creekmur wear?

24. Where did he play collegiate ball?

25. Who had been touted as "the collegiate player of the decade" before entering the NFL?

BARRY SANDERS eludes the outstretched arm of future Hall-of-Famer Reggie White of the Green Bay Packers as he breaks another long gainer for the Lions.

2
Coaches' Corner

A coach is like a lightning rod. He'll be the first to get zapped during stormy weather.

It's his philosophy, his strategies, his personnel, his options. It's his neck, so to speak. Sometimes a coach inherits a bad situation. That doesn't matter. He's still the fall guy after an owner's analysis of the team. (Some win Super Bowls and still get the ax, only to resurface, first on HBO, then in Miami.)

17 men have guided the Detroit Lions over the years. (The total would be 18 when including Hal Griffen's one year as head coach of the Portsmouth Spartans.) Three of them have brought NFL championships to Detroit. Wayne Fontes has coached the most games in the history of the franchise, while John Karcis coached only eight games in 1942, the lowest amount. Here is a look at the Detroit Lions coaches throughout the team's history, including regular season and playoff games. Also included are 10 bonus questions to test your die-hard knowledge of a few of the coaches.

	COACH	YEARS	G	W	L	T	Pct.
1.	Potsy Clark	1934-36, 1940	49	31	15	3	.663
2.	Dutch Clark	1937-38	22	14	8	0	.636
3.	Gus Henderson	1939	11	6	5	0	.545
4.	Bill Edwards	1940-42	14	4	9	1	.321
5.	John Karcis	1942	8	0	8	0	.000
6.	Gus Dorais	1943-47	53	20	31	2	.396
7.	Bo McMillan	1948-50	36	12	24	0	.333
8.	Buddy Parker	1951-56	76	50	24	2	.671
9.	George Wilson	1957-64	106	55	45	6	.547
10.	Harry Gilmer	1965-66	28	10	16	2	.393
11.	Joe Schmidt	1967-72	85	43	35	7	.547
12.	Don McCafferty	1973	14	6	7	1	.464
13.	Rick Forzano	1974-76	32	15	17	0	.469
14.	Tommy Hudspeth	1976-77	24	11	13	0	.458
15.	Monte Clark	1978-84	107	43	63	1	.407
16.	Darryl Rodgers	1985-88	58	18	40	0	.310
17.	Wayne Fontes	1988-present	122	62	60	0	.508
	TOTALS	**1934-95**	**845**	**400**	**420**	**25**	**.488**

TRIVIA QUESTIONS

1. Who coached the College All-Stars to a 6-0 victory over the NFL champion Green Bay Packers in 1937?

2. What was Bo McMillan's middle name?

3. What team did Bo McMillan coach after Detroit?

4. How many games did he coach there?

5. What was Buddy Parker's middle name?

6. What team did Detroit play on December 13, 1964, George Wilson's final game as head coach?

7. What team did the Lions play on December 17, 1972, Joe Schmidt's final game as head coach?

8. What team did Detroit beat in 1995 to make Wayne Fontes the winningest coach in Lions history?

9. Who were the three Lions coaches to win championships?

10. Name the coaches who also played for the Lions during their NFL careers.

3
Grab Bag

This section features miscellaneous trivia as well as some questions that serve as a recap from throughout the history of the Detroit Lions.

1. What are the official colors of the Detroit Lions?

2. What team has Detroit played the most times during the regular season throughout its history?

3. What team has Detroit played the most times in pre-season games?

4. What team has Detroit played the most during the post-season?

5. Name the player who has played the most games as a Lion at 200.

6. What is the name of the Detroit Lions' fight song?

7. Who wrote the song?

8. What two years was Detroit the "City of Champions," with the Lions having won the NFL championship, the Tigers having won the World Series and the Red Wings having won the Stanley Cup in hockey?

9. How many NFL championships have the Lions won?

10. Name the team that has scored the most points ever in one game against the Lions.

11. Name the book about a sportswriter who becomes the last string quarterback for the Detroit Lions during training camp in the early '60s.

12. Who wrote the book?

13. What magazine was he a writer for at the time he wrote the book?

14. What actor played this writer in the film version that came out in 1968?

15. Including the Portsmouth years, what team is the franchise's oldest rival?

16. How many different Lions QBs have thrown for over 3,000 yards in a season?

17. Since 1950, name the only Lions QB who has rushed for over 100 yards in a game.

18. How many Lions QBs have made it to the pro bowl?

19. Name them.

20. How many running backs have made it to the Pro Bowl?

21. Name half of them.

22. Four players have scored 24 points in a game, the highest single game total in franchise history. Name these players.

23. Eddie Murray holds the record for most consecutive field goals in Lions history. How many in a row did he convert from November 13,

1988 until November 12, 1989?

24. How many Heisman Trophy winners have played for the Lions' over the years?

25. Name five of them.

26. Name the last player in the NFL to play without a face mask.

27. Name the three superstars who wore the #20 for Detroit.

28. Name the Lion linebacker who had a role as a gang member in the movie *Motown 9000*, which came out in 1973.

29. Who was William Clay Ford's father?

30. Who was named Lions vice-chairman on February 15, 1995?

31. How many post-season games have the Lions played in, up through the '95 season?

32. This actor wears a Detroit Lions T-shirt during the opening credits of his situation comedy on ABC. Name the actor and the show.

33. How many Lions have had their numbers retired?

34. Name them.

35. How many overall #1 picks have the Lions selected throughout the history of the NFL draft?

THE RECORD BOOK

I
Individual Records

PASSING

Most Completions (Career)
1,074, Bobby Layne, 1950-1958
957, Greg Landry, 1968-1978
952, Gary Danielson, 1976-1984

Most Completions (Season)
346, Scott Mitchell, 1995
252, Gary Danielson, 1984
244, Gary Danielson, 1980

Most Completions (Game)
33, Eric Hipple at Cleveland, 9-28-86
33, Chuck Long vs. Green Bay, 10-25-87

Most Attempts (Career)
2,193, Bobby Layne, 1950-1958
1,747, Greg Landry, 1968-1978
1,684, Gary Danielson, 1976-1984

Most Attempts (Season)
583, Scott Mitchell, 1995
417, Gary Danielson, 1980
416, Chuck Long, 1987

Most Attempts (Game)
  50, Scott Mitchell at Atlanta, November 5, 1995
  50, Scott Mitchell at Washington, October 22, 1995
  50, Eric Hipple at Los Angeles Rams, October 19, 1986

Most Passing Yards (Career)
  15,710, Bobby Layne, 1950-1958
  12,457, Greg Landry, 1968-1978
  11,885, Gary Danielson, 1976-1984

Most Passing Yards (Season)
  4,338, Scott Mitchell, 1995
  3,223, Gary Danielson, 1980
  3,076, Gary Danielson, 1984

Most Passing Yards (Game)
  410, Scott Mitchell vs. Minnesota, November 23, 1995
  374, Bobby Layne vs. Chicago, November 5, 1950
  364, Bobby Layne vs. Pittsburgh, September 27, 1953

Longest Pass Play
  99, Karl Sweetan to Pat Studstill (TD) at Baltimore, Oct. 16, 1966

Most Touchdown Passes (Career)
  118, Bobby Layne, 1950-1958
  80, Greg Landry, 1968-1978
  69, Gary Danielson, 1976-1984

Most Touchdown Passes (Season)
  32, Scott Mitchell, 1995
  26, Bobby Layne, 1951
  24, Earl Morrall, 1963

Most Touchdown Passes (Game)
  5, Gary Danielson vs.Minnesota, December 9, 1978

Most Passes Intercepted (Career)
142, Bobby Layne 1950-1958
87, Milt Plum, 1962-1967
81, Greg Landry, 1968-1978

Most Passes Intercepted (Season)
23, Bobby Layne, 1951
23, Jeff Komlo, 1979
21, Bobby Layne, 1953

Most Passes Intercepted (Game)
7, Frank Sinkwich vs. Green Bay, October 24, 1943

RUSHING

Most Attempts (Career)
2,077, Barry Sanders, 1989-1995
1,203, Dexter Bussey, 1974-1984
1,165, Altie Taylor, 1969-1976
1,131, Billy Sims, 1980-1984

Most Attempts (Season)
342, Barry Sanders, 1991
331, Barry Sanders, 1994
314, Barry Sanders, 1995
313, Billy Sims, 1980

Most Attempts (Game)
40, Barry Sanders at Dallas, September 19, 1994
36, Billy Sims at Green Bay, November 20, 1983
36, James Jones vs. Miami, October 27, 1985
36, James Jones at Minnesota, September 7, 1986

Most Rushing Yards (Career)
10,172, Barry Sanders, 1989-1995
5,106, Billy Sims, 1980-1984
5,105, Dexter Bussey, 1974-1984
4,279, Altie Taylor, 1969-1976
3,933, Nick Pietrosante, 1959-1965

Most Rushing Yards (Season)
1,883, Barry Sanders, 1994
1,548, Barry Sanders, 1991
1,500, Barry Sanders, 1995
1,470, Barry Sanders, 1989
1,437, Billy Sims, 1981

Most Rushing Yards (Game)
237, Barry Sanders vs. Tampa Bay, November 13, 1994
220, Barry Sanders at Minnesota, November 24, 1991
198, Bob Hoernschemeyer vs. NY Yanks, November 23, 1950

Longest Rushing Plays
96, Bob Hoernschemeyer (TD) vs. NY Yanks, November 23, 1950
85, Barry Sanders at Tampa Bay, October 2, 1994
85, Bob Hoernschemeyer (TD) vs. Green Bay, November 22, 1951

Most Rushing Touchdowns (Career)
73, Barry Sanders, 1989-1995
42, Billy Sims, 1980-1984
28, Nick Pietrosante, 1959-1965
26, Mel Farr, 1967-1973

Most Rushing Touchdowns (Season)
16, Barry Sanders, 1991
14, Barry Sanders, 1989
13, Barry Sanders, 1990
13, Billy Sims, 1980 and 1981

Most Rushing Touchdowns (Game)
4, Barry Sanders at Minnesota, November 24, 1991

RECEIVING

Most Receptions (Career)
336, Charlie Sanders, 1968-1977
334, Brett Perriman, 1991-1995
325, Gail Cogdill, 1960-1968
318, Herman Moore, 1991-1995

Most Receptions (Season)
123, Herman Moore, 1995
108, Brett Perriman, 1995
77, James Jones, 1984
72, Herman Moore, 1994

Most Receptions (Game)
14, Herman Moore vs. Chicago, December 4, 1995
12, Brett Perriman vs. Minnesota, November 23, 1995
12, Brett Perriman at Chicago, November 19, 1995
12, James Jones at Cleveland, September 28, 1986
12, Cloyce Box at Baltimore, December 3, 1950

Most Receiving Yards (Career)
5,220, Gail Cogdill, 1960-1968
4,895, Herman Moore, 1991-1995
4,817, Charlie Sanders, 1968-1977
4,682, Leonard Thompson, 1975-1986
4,223, Brett Perriman, 1991-1995

Most Receiving Yards (Season)
1,686, Herman Moore, 1995
1,488, Brett Perriman, 1995

1,266, Pat Studstill, 1966
1,173, Herman Moore, 1994
1,091, Richard Johnson, 1989

Most Receiving Yards (Game)
302, Cloyce Box vs. Baltimore, December 3, 1950
248, Richard Johnson vs. New Orleans, December 3, 1989
202, Cloyce Box vs. Dallas, December 13, 1952
183, Herman Moore vs. Chicago, December 4, 1995

Most Receiving Touchdowns (Career)
35, Herman Moore, 1991-1995
35, Terry Barr, 1957-1965
35, Leonard Thompson, 1975-1986
32, Cloyce Box, 1949-1950, 1952-1954

Most Receiving Touchdowns (Season)
15, Cloyce Box, 1952
14, Herman Moore, 1995
13, Terry Barr, 1963
12, Leon Hart, 1951

Most Receiving Touchdowns (Game)
4, Cloyce Box vs. Baltimore, December 3, 1950—3 from Layne, 1 from Fred Enke

KICKING

Most Field Goals (Career)
244, Eddie Murray, 1980-1991
141, Errol Mann, 1969-1976
101, Jason Hanson, 1992-1995

Most Field Goals (Season)
34, Jason Hanson, 1993
28, Jason Hanson, 1995
27, Eddie Murray, 1980

Most Field Goals (Game)
6, Garo Yepremian at Minnesota, November 13, 1966

Longest Field Goal
56, Jason Hanson vs. Cleveland, October 8, 1995

Most Extra Points (Career)
384, Eddie Murray, 1980-1991
213, Errol Mann, 1969-1976
183, Doak Walker, 1950-1955

Most Extra Points (Season)
48, Jason Hanson, 1995
46, Eddie Murray, 1981
43, Doak Walker, 1951 and 1954

Most Extra Points (Game)
8, Jim Martin vs. Cleveland, December 29, 1957

SCORING

Most Total Touchdowns (Career)
80, Barry Sanders, 1989-1995
47, Billy Sims, 1980-1984
38, Terry Barr, 1957-1965
38, Leonard Thompson, 1975-1986

Most Total Touchdowns (Season)
17, Barry Sanders, 1991

16, Barry Sanders, 1990
16, Billy Sims, 1980

Most Total Touchdowns (Game)
4, Barry Sanders at Minnesota, November 24, 1991—all four rushing
4, Cloyce Box at Baltimore, December 3, 1950—all four receiving
4, Dutch Clark vs. Brooklyn, October 22, 1934—all four rushing

Most Points Scored (Career)
1,113, Eddie Murray, 1980-1991
636, Errol Mann, 1969-1976
534, Doak Walker, 1950-1955
448, Jason Hanson, 1992-1995

Most Points Scored (Season)
132, Jason Hanson, 1995
130, Jason Hanson, 1993
128, Doak Walker, 1950

Most Points Scored (Game)
24, Barry Sanders at Minnesota, November 24, 1991
24, Cloyce Box at Baltimore, December 3, 1950
24, Doak Walker at Green Bay, November 19, 1950
24, Dutch Clark vs. Brooklyn, October 22, 1934

SACKS

Most Sacks (Career)
75.5, Al Baker, 1978-1982
63.0, Michael Cofer, 1983-1992
61.0, William Gay, 1978-1987

Most Sacks (Season)
23.0, Al Baker, 1978

18.0, Al Baker, 1980
16.0, Al Baker, 1979

Most Sacks (Game)
5.5, William Gay at Tampa Bay, September 4, 1983
5.0, Al Baker vs. Tampa Bay, November 12, 1978

INTERCEPTIONS

Most Interceptions (Career)
62, Dick LeBeau, 1959-1972
56, Lem Barney, 1967-1977
50, Yale Lary, 1952-1953, 1956-1964

Most Interceptions (Season)
12, Don Doll, 1950
12, Jack Christiansen, 1953
11, Don Doll, 1949

Most Interceptions (Game)
4, Don Doll at Chicago Cardinals, October 23, 1949

Longest Interception Return
102, Bob Smith at Chicago Bears, November 24, 1949

2
Team Records

SEASON

Most Passing Completions
362, 1995 (16 Games)

Most Passing Attempts
605, 1995 (16 Games)

Most Passing Yards
4,360, 1995 (16 Games)

Most Rushing Attempts
596, 1981 (16 Games)

Most Rushing Yards
2,885, 1936 (12 Games)

Most Total Yards
6,113, 1995 (16 Games)

Most Touchdowns Scored
48, 1995 (16 Games)

Most Points Scored
436, 1995 (16 Games)

Least Yards Allowed on Defense
2,722, 1982 (16 Games)

Most Sacks (Defense)
55, 1978 (16 Games) for 482 yards

Most Passes Intercepted
38, 1953 (12 Games)

GAME - Offense

Most Net Yards Passing
395 vs. Minnesota, November 23, 1995

Most Net Yards Rushing
426 vs. Pittsburgh, November 4, 1934

Most Total Yards
582 (205 passing, 377 rushing) vs. NY Yanks, Nov. 23, 1950

Most Points Scored
59 vs. Cleveland, December 29, 1957 (NFL Championship Game)

GAME - Defense

Fewest Rushing Yards Allowed
-3 at Pittsburgh, November 9, 1952

Fewest Passing Yards Allowed
-31 at Tampa Bay, September 9, 1978

Fewest Total Yards Allowed
14 at Chicago Cardinals, September 15, 1940

Most Total Yards Allowed
676 (482 passing, 194 rushing) vs. Washington (OT), Nov. 4, 1990

Most Sacks
11 at Philadelphia, November 16, 1986
11 at Green Bay, November 7, 1965
11 vs. Green Bay, November 22, 1962

Most Takeaways (Total)
10 (5 fumble recoveries, 5 interceptions) vs. Minnesota, Dec. 9, 1962

Most Interceptions
 8 vs. Chicago Bears, September 22, 1968

3
Lions vs. the League

Opponents (1934-1995)	Regular Season W	L	T
Arizona Cardinals	1	0	0
Chicago Cardinals	19	9	3
St. Louis Cardinals	5	4	0
Phoenix Cardinals	1	2	0
Total Cardinals	26	15	3
Atlanta Falcons	18	6	0
Baltimore Ravens	0	0	0
Cleveland Browns	12	3	0
Total Ravens	12	3	0
Baltimore Colts (First)	1	0	0
Boston Yanks	3	2	0
Brooklyn Dodgers	8	3	0
Buffalo Bills	3	1	1
Card-Pitt (1944)	2	0	0
Carolina Panthers	0	0	0
Chicago Bears	50	70	3
Cincinnati Bengals	3	3	0
Cincinnati-St. Louis Gunners	2	0	0
Dallas Cowboys	6	7	0
Dallas Texans	2	0	0
Denver Broncos	3	4	0

Green Bay Packers	56	63	6
Houston Oilers	3	4	0
Indianapolis Colts	1	1	0
Baltimore Colts (Second)	16	16	2
Total Colts	17	17	2
Jacksonville Jaguars	1	0	0
Kansas City Chiefs	3	4	0
Miami Dolphins	2	3	0
Minnesota Vikings	25	42	2
New England Patriots	3	3	0
New Orleans Saints	6	7	1
New York Bulldogs	1	0	0
New York Giants	14	12	1
New York Jets	4	3	0
New York Yanks	2	1	1
Oakland Raiders	2	2	0
Los Angeles Raiders	0	3	0
Total Raiders	2	5	0
Philadelphia Eagles	12	9	2
Phil-Pitt Steagles (1943)	0	1	0
Pittsburgh Steelers (Pirates)	13	12	1
San Diego Chargers	3	2	0
San Francisco 49ers	26	27	1
St. Louis Rams	0	0	0
Cleveland Rams	8	7	0
Los Angeles Rams	28	32	1
Total Rams	36	39	1
Seattle Seahawks	2	4	0
Tampa Bay Buccaneers	19	17	0

Washington Redskins	3	23	0
Boston Redskins	3	0	0
Total Redskins	6	23	0

Post-Season

Opponent	W	L
Cleveland Browns	3	1
Dallas Cowboys	1	1
Green Bay Packers	0	2
Los Angeles Rams	1	0
New York Giants	1	0
Philadelphia Eagles	0	1
San Francisco 49ers	1	1
Washington Redskins	0	2
Totals	**7**	**8**

THE ANSWERS

LIONS HISTORY & TRIVIA

Through the Years

1 - Hail the Colors Blue and Silver(1930-34) The Portsmouth Years

1. Purple
2. George
3. Butler University
4. Roy Lumpkin
5. 1) Father 2) Ramblin N' Wreck
6. Georgia Tech
7. Ironton (Ohio) Tanks
8. They were fined for having players on their rosters who were ineligible to play pro ballbecause they hadnot yet graduated from college.
9. $1,000
10. 1) Dutch Clark, tailback 2.) George Christensen, tackle
11. The Spartans claimed to have had a game against Green Bay scheduled for December 13 in Portsmouth. It was not on the league schedule, but had been agreed to after the schedule was out. Green Bay refused to play the game. Joe Carr, president of the NFL, ruled that since it was a tentative agreement, either team had the right to back out. Since Portsmouth finished at 11-3 and the Packers were 12-2, Carr awarded the title to Green Bay. Portsmouth claimed they tied for the title since a true champion was not determined on the field.
12. Clare Randolph
13. The game was played indoors at Chicago Stadium. The width of the playing field was 45 yards, while the length was 80.
14. Heavy snow and freezing temperatures made it impossible to play outside. With the weather still bad late in the week, the Spartans agreed to play the game indoors.
15. 55 points (six TDs, three FGs, 10 PATs)

When the Lions Came to Town

1. The annual baseball meetings
2. Richards and the syndicate paid a fee of $15,000. (They also paid off the previous owners' debts of $7,952.08)
3. 26
4. He conducted a contest on his radio station to name the Detroit team.
5. The name "Lions" corresponded well with the jungle cat nickname of the Tigers.
6. Cy Huston
7. With so many area auto executives in the syndicate, Fox joked that Potsy would have a hard time choosing what namebrand automobile to own.
8. 25,000
9. Two years

10. $1.10
11. 10 cents
12. Green Bay Packers, Chicago Bears, Chicago Cardinals, Cincinnati Reds
13. Grid and Iron
14. The zoo's famous chimp, Jo Mendi
15. William "Moon" Baker, William Bone, Gerald Polsin, Judy Tosha
16. Baker—in Richards's opinion, he fit the role of a Lion best since he could roar the loudest.
17. 45
18. 25
19. "Fair and Square Club"
20. He also served as the team's unofficial scout.
21. Doc Holland

The First Season
1. The Traverse City Athletic Club
2. Paul Whiteman
3. The New York Giants
4. 9-0 (Detroit). Dutch Clark kicked a 20-yard field goal and Roy Lumpkin added a 45-yard interception return for a TD.
5. Glenn Presnell kicked a 54-yard field goal. (It stood as an NFL record for 19 years.)
6. They won their first 10 games before losing to Green Bay at home, 3-0.
7. Seven
8. Pittsburgh Pirates
9. 426 yards (a team record)
10. The game was played in Portsmouth on October 28. The Lions beat the Cincinnati Reds, 38-0.
11. 194 yards
12. The Old Newsboys Goodfellow Fund
13. Eight
14. $4,000
15. $2,200
16. Three (two from Presnell, one from Ernie Cadell)
17. Dutch Clark and George Christensen
18. Leroy
19. Russia
20. "Ox"

21. "Tarzan"
22. "Big John"
23. Nebraska
24. Oregon
25. Stanford
26. Illinois
27. Three
28. Five
29. One
30. Zero

2 - Not Queen, Not Duke, Not Prince (1935-39)
1. None
2. -72
3. The Lions were the only team to score a touchdown in every one of their 12 games.
4. Nine
5. Ernie Cadell (Eight)
6. Bill Shepherd
7. Boston Redskins
8. Ernie Cadell
9. Ernie Cadell (450 yards), Dutch Clark (412 yards), Bill Shepherd (425 yards, some with Boston) and Ace Gutowsky (295 yards)
10. Three
11. Dutch Clark
12. Five
13. The Lions and the College All-Stars tied, 7-7.
14. "Red"
15. He booted the longest punt in team history, 85 yards during a 38-0 victory.
16. Dutch Clark and "Ox" Emerson
17. 2,885 yards
18. The record is five straight road games. The streak began at Philadelphia on October 11.
19. Two wins, three losses
20. 1) rushing attempts; 2) rushing yards; 3) rushing average; 4) rushing TDs; 5) offensive TDs; 6) first downs; 7) fewest fumbles
21. 827 yards
22. it was a record for 24 years.
23. Four
24. Six
25. Sid Wagner—a guard at Michigan State

26. Steve Hannigan
27. None
28. The Lions beat the Dodgers, 30-0.
29. Vern Huffman
30. Green Bay twice and the Bears twice
31. Vern Huffman (two)
32. Four
33. 12
34. Lloyd Cardwell
35. Bud Shaver
36. 55 cents
37. Washington won, 7-5
38. Lloyd Cardwell (30 points)
39. Center and linebacker
40. Byron "Whizzer" White (from Pittsburgh)
41. Elmer
42. "Gloomy Gus"
43. Ernie Cadell
44. Brooklyn Dodgers
45. He was sold to the Brooklyn Dodgers.
46. 445 yards (1938) and 420 yards (1939)
47. Chuck Hanneman (29 points)
48. Dwight Sloan
49. His three interceptions in 102 attempts set a team record for fewest interceptions in one season by a Lions QB.
50. George Richards had reportedly paid a college player $100 to pay for dental work. In return, the player agreed to tell NFL scouts for other teams that he was not interested in playing pro ball. On draft day, coach Henderson assumed that the player was set to play for the Lions, so he passed over him in the first round. In a move of revenge for past incidents, George Halas, who had found out about the deal, chose the player for the Bears with their first round draft pick. Richards was upset over losing the player he thought he had and even angrier about Henderson's poor judgment. As a result, Gus had a one year coaching career in Detroit.
51. Clyde "Bulldog" Turner
52. He played center at Hardin-Simmons.
53. Joe Carr fined the Lions $5,000 for tampering with "Bulldog" Turner while he was still in school.
54. Doyle Nave—a back from USC
55. Zero
56. Centenary
57. Oregon
58. Arkansas
59. Indiana
60. West Maryland

3 - The Lion in Winter (1940-49)
1. Bill Alfs
2. Oxford in England
3. $15,000
4. White would stand off to the side of where the punt was going to land, so he could entice the defenders away from the ball. Then he would move to the ball at the last moment and catch it on the run.
5. He earned a bronze star.
6. Coach Potsy Clark (Even owner Mandel registered.)
7. 14 yards (a team record)
8. Turnovers—the Lions fumbled eight times
9. "Whizzer" White
10. Potsy stepped down to become the athletic director at Grand Rapids University in Michigan.
11. Western Reserve University in Cleveland
12. He set a then team record for longest kickoff return for a TD at 101 yards.
13. He intercepted a pass and returned it 51 yards for a TD. He threw a 23 yard pass to Bill Fisk for a TD. The Lions won, 21-3.
14. 24
15. White, Andy Logan, Cotton Price, Owen Thurek, Floyd Parsons
16. John Tripson won the Navy Cross, and Maurice Britt won the prestigious Medal of Honor.
17. Eight
18. The score was All-Stars 12, Lions 0.
19 He joined the marines.
20. "Bull"
21. At the time, Hackney established a team record for longest rushing play from scrimmage at 78 yards.
22. Five

23. 263 points
24. Bill Fisk
25. Four
26. He returned three kicks for 30 yards.
27. Charles
28. Five years
29. Notre Dame
30. Knute Rockne
31. The game was the last 0-0 tie in NFL history.
32. Georgia
33. He was released due to high blood pressure and a heart murmur.
34. Four days
35. He won the NFL's Outstanding Rookie of the Year Award.
36. He was discharged because he had flat feet.
37. He was the first Lion to throw four TDs in one game.
38. Don Hutson
39. Vince Lombardi
40. Seven
41. Otto Graham of Northwestern. (Before he could join the Lions, he was called into military service and later chose to play for the Cleveland Browns of the AAC. He never played for Detroit.)
42. Chester Wetterland and Alex Ketzko
43. John Greene
44. Four
45. Bill Radovich
46. Harry Hopp
47. "Hippity"
48. Russell Thomas
49. Philadelphia Eagles
50. He kicked an 81-yard punt. (It ranks second on the team's all-time list.)
51. The Boston Yanks
52. Dave Ryan
53. Bob Cifers, Paul White and the Lions' first draft choice in 1948.
54. Seven months
55. $20,000
56. "Bullet"
57. He was the league's MVP.
58. Glenn Davis (He had a commitment with the army and never played with the Lions.)
59. "Gabby"
60. Clyde Leforce
61. Bill Dudley scored 66 points for the '47 season.
62. Bill Dudley
63. $100
64. Frank Leahy
65. Alvin
66. Five years
67. Fred Enke
68. Y. A. Tittle—QB from Louisiana State. (He never played for the Lions, opting to play for the Baltimore Colts of the AAC. He later went on to become a legendary QB with the San Francisco 49ers and New York Giants.)
69. Les Bingaman
70. Bob Mann and Mel Groomes
71. Joe Margucci
72. Camp Wilson
73. Jim Gillette
74. Cloyce box
75. Halfback
76. Bob Smith
77. Nine
78. Four
79. Nick Kerbawy
80. 81 points
81. Johnny Rauch—QB from Georgia
82. New York Bulldogs
83. Fred Enke, Clyde LeForce, Frank Tripuka
84. Bob Mann (1,014 yards in 1949)
85. 66
86. Colorado
87. Nebraska
88. Ohio State
89. Tulsa
90. Michigan

4 - Life in the Fast Layne (1950-57)
1. New York Bulldogs
2. Camp Wilsom
3. Bob Mann
4. Leon Hart

5. 1) New York Giants; 2) Chicago Bears; 3) New York Bulldogs; 4) Chicago Cardinals
6. Brooklyn Dodgers and Chicago Hornets
7. Chicago Cardinals
8. "Fum"
9. Six (1950-1955)
10. Washington Redskins
11. Wally Triplett (Lions lost, 65-24)
12. Bob Hoernschemeyer
13. 302 yards
14. 50
15. Tom Fears
16. Doak Walker
17. Don Doll
18. Highland Park High School in Dallas, Texas
19. Raymond
20. One year
21. "Hunchy"
22. Cloyce Box, Jim Cain, Wally Triplett
23. Johnny Panelli (plus a second round draft pick)
24. Emerson Cole
25. Doak Walker
26. Dick Stanfel
27. Jack Christiansen
28. Leon Hart (35 receptions)
29. 26
30. He scouted the Lions' upcoming opponents.
31. "Sherriff"
32. He campaigned for sherriff of Milwaukee in the 1952 city elections.
33. Third
34. 22nd
35. Eight (1952-1959)
36. The U. S. Open Golf Tournament
37. Jug Girard
38. 1) Green Bay Packers; 2) Defensive back
39. Earl
40. James Hardy
41. Buster Ramsey
42. The player was halfback Jerry Krall who had become a free agent at the end of the previous season. Nick Kerbawy, the Lions' GM, had to drive to Toledo personally to sign Krall, then he had to pre-date the contract to make it appear legitimate.
43. San Francisco 49ers
44. 52
45. Pittsburgh Steelers
46. Jack Christiansen
47. Most receiving TDs in a season (15)
48. Jim Doran
49. The President's Trophy
50. The College All-Stars
51. Harley Sewell
52. Seven
53. Dick Flanagan
54. Lew Carpenter
55. Gene Gedman
56. Jim David
57. Wide receiver Tom Fears (He suffered a cracked vertebra on the play.)
58. Chris's Crew(Named after Jack Christiansen)
59. 12
60. 38
61. Washington Redskins
62. 1) Yale Lary; 2) Lew Carpenter; 3) Bob Hoernschemeyer
63. He became an NFL game official.
64. Ramsey won the bet since Bingaman's 349 1/2 pound weight was closer to 300.
65. Yale Lary and Gene Gedman
66. Hoernschemeyer
67. Bill Bowman
68. The Cleveland Indians were playing a home game in the World Series on October 3. The Browns would not agree to move the site of the game to Briggs Stadium, so the game was postponed until December 19.
69. He was referring to Doak Walker, who had scored 18 points and totaled 194 yards in a game against the 49ers in 1954.
70. Tom Dublinski
71. Philadelphia Eagles
72. Dorne Dibble
73. Tom Dublinski
74. Joe Schmidt
75. Lew Carpenter (543 yards)
76. Fullback

77. Gene Gedman (479 yards)
78. Dave Middleton
79. Chicago Bears
80. 44
81. John Henry Johnson
82. Tobin Rote and Val Joe Walker
83. John Henry Johnson (621 yards)
84. QB Earl Morrall and a 1959 and 1960 draft pick
85. 22
86. 37
87. 80
88. 14
89. 56
90. 82
91. 28
92. 24
93. 65
94. 25
95. Wisconsin
96. West Texas State
97. Illinois
98. Colorado A & M
99. Indiana
100. Notre Dame

5 - Mad Duck But No Glory (1958-1970)
1. George
2. Gary, Indiana
3. Emerson High School
4. Iowa
5. The Outland Trophy
6. "Tippy Toes"
7. He bartended at Detroit's Lindell Athletic Club and became a professional wrestler. (He actually had a share of the ownership of the bar which he had to sell in order to be reinstated by NFL Commissioner Pete Rozelle.)
8. "Webster"
9. Georgian Bay
10. Dick LeBeau
11. 62
12. The Detroit Pistons of the NBA
13. Terry Barr (92 yards) and Gene Gedman (12 yards)
14. Toronto Argonaughts
15. St. Louis Cardinals
16. Gerald Perry
17. LA Rams
18. Fourth
19. Sixth
20. Nick Pietrosante
21. Don Shula
22. Jim Martin
23. 1) John Hadl; 2) Eddie Wilson
24. Jim Ninowski, Hopalong Cassady, and Bill Glass
25. 10 (five INTs, five fumble recoveries)
26. The Huntley-Brinkley Report on NBC-TV
27. Terry Barr (13) and Gail Cogdill (10)
28. Yale Lary
29. Pete Beathard
30. Russ Thomas
31. 19th round (in '63)
32. Hampton Institute (Virginia)
33. He was suspended for fighting.
34. Van Patrick
35. Alex Karras, Roger Brown, Darris McCord and Sam Williams
36. True (in 1965)
37. Fred Biletnikoff
38. 18th
39. Ron Kramer
40. Backup QB
41. Minnesota Vikings
42. Dennis Gaubatz
43. He claimed he was injured after someone stepped on his back.
44. Karras
45. Atlanta Falcons
46. He was suspended from February to May in '66 formaking comments about Gilmer while speaking to a women's group in Flint, Michigan. An excerpt:"Gilmer doesn't know how to handle men andhe's not ready for a coaching job ... If Gilmer comes back at all, he might be the only one." Cogdill was also fined $1,000.
47. Garo Yepremian

48. Six
49. LA Rams
50. 34
51. Bill McPeak and Chuck Knox
52. Jim Martin and Jim David
53. Pat Studstill
54. Ninth
55. Errol Mann
56. Mel Farr
57. Lem Barney
58. Bill Munson
59. The college draft of 1968 caused Schmidt to quit momentarily. Schmidt wanted to draft RB Mike Hill from USC, but Ford and Russ Thomas decided on taking QB Greg Landry with the team's number one pick. Schmidt returned after collecting himself.
60. Bobby Layne
61. Most team INTs in a game (eight)
62. Dick Butkus
63. Alex Karras and Lem Barney
64. Steve Owens
65. Tom Dempsey
66. Washington Redskins (He quit football and pursued a career in show business.)
67. Notre Dame
68. Tennessee
69. UCLA
70. Penn State
71. Houston
72. Tennessee
73. No college
74. Oklahoma
75. Washington State
76. Michigan
77. 47
78. 24
79. 16
80. 52
81. 89

6 - Look Homeward, Leo (1970-79)
1. Philadelphia Eagles
2. "Coyote"

3. Lee Trevino
4. Ron Jessie
5. 97 yards
6. Steve Owens
7. Second (behind John Brockington of Green Bay)
8. Eight
9. 530 yards
10. Errol Mann
11. North Dakota
12. "The Pearl"
13. Second
14. Eight (1972-79)
15. Dick LeBeau and Wayne Walker
16. LeBeau owns the career INT mark with 62 and Walker holds the record for most games played as a Lion at 200.
17. 18
18. Nine
19. Baltimore Colts
20. 1971 against the Dallas Cowboys. (The score was 16-13 in favor of the Colts.)
21. Raymond Barry
22. Dick Jauron
23. Charlie Weaver
24. The Naval Academy
25. Third
26. He was undrafted in '74, but signed as a free agent in 1976.
27. Sam Wyche
28. Houston Oilers
29. Houston gave up a fourth round pick to the Lions and Detroit received defensive back Ben Davis from Cleveland.
30. Denver Broncos
31. Thanksgiving (Nov. 28, 1974)
32. 31-27 (Denver)
33. Altie Taylor
34. Second
35. The Pontiac Metropolitan Stadium (PonMet)
36. According to the Detroit Lions' Media Guide, the seating capacity is 80,368
37. $55.7 million
38. The Main Event Sports Bar and Grill

39. Kansas City Chiefs (Lions won 27-24)
40. Dallas Cowboys (Dallas won 36-10)
41. Chicago Bears (The score was 27-7.)
42. Joe Reed
43. Errol Mann
44. Seven and a half (1969-half of 1976)
45. First
46. 636
47. Benny Ricardo
48. Charlie Weaver
49. A team record 67 sacks
50. Weaver
51. Cleveland Browns
52. 11 (1966-1976)
53. 306
54. Eddie Payton
55. James Hunter
56. Horace King
57. 336
58. Seven
59. 31
60. "The Silver Rush"
61. Doug English, Al Baker, Dave Pureifory, Charlie Weaver, Ed O'Neil and John Woodcock
62. "Bubba"
63. 23
64. The Bucs had -31 yards passing for the game.
65. 55
66. 12 (1967-78)
67. Baltimore Colts
68. Twice (1978 and 1979)
69. Jeff Komlo
70. 23
71. Minnesota
72. USC
73. Tennessee
74. Massachusetts
75. Oklahoma

7 - A Sooner in Lions Clothing (1980-1983)
1. San Francisco 49ers
2. Doug English (He came back one year later.)
3. Hooks High School in Texas
4. His old high school jersey

5. Three
6. 153 yards
7. 1,303 yards
8. 16 (13 rushing, three receiving)
9. Atlanta Falcons
10. Eddie Murray
11. 116
12. Seventh
13. 3,223 yards
14. Tom Skladany
15. 18
16. Wide Receiver Mark Nichols
17. Freddie Scott
18. Jeff Komlo
19. San Francisco 49ers
20. The replay showed that the Lions had 12 men on the field during the play, but the league did not change the result of the game.
21. 596
22. 1,437
23. 15 (13 rushing, two receiving)
24. Fred Scott (1981—1,022 yards)
25. Dave Pureifory
26. Five (1978-82)
27. Rushing yards (2,795) and rushing TDs (26—tied with San Diego)
28. San Francisco defeated Cincinnati, 26-21.
29. San Francisco
30. Keith Dorney
31. James Hunter
32. 19 yards
33. Al Baker, Dave Pureifory and William Gay
34. Houston Gamblers
35 $4.5 million
36. Linebacker Stan White
37. Baltimore Colts
38. St. Louis Cardinals
39. LA Rams
40. Four
41. 36
42. 189
43. Cincinnati Bengals (Lions lost, 17-9.)
44. Fewest points allowed (286)
45. William Gay

46. Dexter Bussey
47. Lions Man of the Year and Michigander of the year
48. Three
49. Three
50. Mike Black
51. Philadelphia Eagles
52. Five
53. Six wins, two losses
54. Bruce McNorton
55. Alvin Hall
56. ken Fantetti
57. 24
58. 78
59. 57
60. 79
61. Utah State
62. Texas
63. Wyoming
64. Colorado State
65. USC
66. Amherst
67. Texas Arlington
68. Purdue

8 - The Seven Year Drought (1984-1990)
1. 103
2. 5,106
3. Dexter Bussey
4. 5,105
5. 81 yards
6. 42
7. James Jones
8. 77
9. San Francisco won, 30-27, on a last second field goal by Ray Wersching.
10. Angelo King
11. Three
12. He threw for 3,076 yards. It was the second time in his career that he passed for 3,000+ yards in a single season.
13. Michigan State and Arizona State
14. Lomas Brown
15. Joe Ferguson

16. Buffalo Bills
17. Wilbert Montgomery
18. Cleveland's third round pick in the 1986 draft
19. Pete Mandley
20. Leonard Thompson
21. 12 (1975-86)
22. Steve Mott
23. Alabama
24. "The Leopard"
25. Doug English
26. Jimmy Giles
27. Harvey Salem
28. James Jones
29. He set a team record with 33 completions in the game.
30. Chuck Long
31. Iowa
32. Leonard Thompson
33. Tampa Bay (Lions won, 38-17.)
34. Jeff Chadwick
35. 35
36. Jerry Ball
37. Chicago Bears (It would have been a home game.)
38. Three
39. Todd Hons
40. Mike Black
41. 20
42. Jim Arnold
43. Rusty Hilger
44. Los Angeles Raiders
45. Green Bay Packers in Milwaukee (Lions won the game, 19-9.)
46. Darrell "Mouse" Davis
47. Rusty Hilger
48. "The Silver Stretch"
49. New Orleans Saints
50. Sixth ('89 Draft)
51. Bob Gagliano
52. Richard Johnson
53. 1,091
54. 248
55. 23
56. 14

57. 21
58. James Wilder
59. Dan Owens (second round) and Marc Spindler (third round)
60. 674 yards
61. Michael Cofer
62. Tulane
63. Florida
64. Tennessee
65. USC

9 - The House That Wayne Built (1991-Present)
1. Michigan State
2. Defensive back
3. New York Jets
4. One—1962 (His playing career ended after he suffered a broken leg.)
5. Visitation High School (Bay City, Mich.)
6. John McKay
7. Tampa Bay
8. 1985
9. Five
10. Barry Sanders, Chris Spielman, Jerry Ball, Lomas Brown and Mel Gray
11. Charlie Sanders
12. Eric Andolsek
13. Washington State
14. 60
15. Third
16. Louisiana State
17. 65
18. 50
19. New Orleans Saints
20. He became the first player in NFL history to lead the league in punt return average (15.4 yards) and kickoff return average (25.8 yards).
21. NFC 21, AFC 15
22. Six
23. Jerry Ball, Lomas Brown, Barry Sanders, Chris Spielman, Bennie Blades and Mel Gray
24. 1,113
25. Jason Hanson
26. Bennie Blades
27. Pat Swilling
28. New Orleans
29. Ryan McNeil (second round)
30. Derrick Moore
31. Eric Lynch
32. Ty Hallock
33. Robert Porcher
34. 130
35. Three
36. Lomas Brown, Barry Sanders and Pat Swilling
37. Dave Krieg (It was an incomplete pass.)
38. Cleveland Browns
39. 6' 6"
40. William Scott Mitchell
41. Fourth
42. Orlando Thunder
43. Atlanta Falcons
44. Anthony Carter
45. His wife Angela
46. Miami Dolphins
47. Dallas Cowboys ('92 playoff game)
48. Jason Hanson
49. Luther Ellis
50. 56 yards
51. 123
52. 108
53. 32
54. 4,338
55. 14
56. 132
57. Florida
58. Ohio State
59. Miami
60. Oklahoma State
61. Virginia
62. Washington State
63. Maryland
64. Utah
65. USC

10 - Championship Games
1. Their pass defense
2. Six
3. All 23 players
4. Buddy Parker

5. Dutch Clark(80 yards)
6. The "Ed Thorp Memorial Trophy"
7. $300
8. Each of the three players blocked a punt in the game.
9. They removed the leather covering off the ball and sliced it into 26 equal segments. The segments were mounted on scrolls and handed out to the players, Potsy Clark, the team's trainer/equipment manager Abe Kushner and Dr. Carl Joseph.
10. Detroit was favored by three and a half points.
11. Pat Harder and Vince Banonis
12. 1947 and 1948
13. Jim Martin
14. Though Otto Graham's pass to Pete Brewster was completed in the end zone, it was ruled illegal because an ineligible receiver had tipped the ball.
15. 97
16. 59
17. Cleveland was favored by three and a half points.
18. Joe Schmidt
19. Six
20. Carl Karlivacz
21. 95
22. Nine (four for Graham)
23. Two (From 45 and 33 yards)
24. Two
25. Otto Graham (He would be back for one more year.)
26. Joe Schmidt
27. Bill Bowman
28. Tom Dublinski
29. Terry Barr
30. Lew Carpenter
31. The QB was third stringer Jerry Reichow and the receiver was Hopalong Cassady.
32. 26, 78, 23 and 32 yards
33. Steve Junker
34. 280 yards
35. Brown said: "It didn't happen on the field. It was last summer when the Detroit Lions obtained Tobin Rote from Green Bay."

11 - The Thanksgiving Day Tradition
1. Graham McNamee (play by play) and Don Wilson (color commentary)
2. Five
3. Cleveland Browns (Browns won, 28-21)
4. Boston Yanks (Lions lost, 34-10)
5. Bob Hoernschemeyer
6. Jack Christiansen
7. 1950-1955
8. 110 yards
9. Sam Williams scored on a 6-yard fumble recovery.
10. 13-13 tie
11. "The Mud Bowl"
12. 1951 (against Green Bay)
13. Oakland Raiders
14. 43
15. LA Rams(Lions lost, 20-0)
16. Doug English
17. Once (It was a 20-0 victory over the Bears in 1979.)
18. Dave Williams
19. Leonard Thompson
20. Cleveland Browns
21. He scored his 50th career rushing TD in the game.
22. 351 yards
23. 410 yards
24. Brett Perriman
25. Seven

Profiles

1 - Dutch Clark
1. Fowler, Colorado
2. Harry
3. Seven
4. 21 games
5. Three (1932, 1935 and 1936)
6. 11-20-2
7. 15
8. Six seasons
9. 369
10. 1951

2 - Bobby Layne
1. Santa Anna, Texas
2. Lawrence
3. Doak Walker
4. 28 wins, 0 losses
5. 11 of 12
6. He was not interested in playing with Pittsburgh because they ran a single-wing offense. Layne had been thriving under a T-wing formation at Texas.
7. Clyde "Bulldog" Turner
8. Sid Luckman and Johnny Lujack
9. $50,000
10. "Slim" (This was because Layne did not have a slightly protruding stomach his first year in Detroit.)
11. *Time*
12. Joe Schmidt
13. 97 yards (to Cloyce Box on Nov. 23, 1953 vs. Green Bay)
14. Sewell was a fellow graduate of the University of Texas.
15. 1956
16. George Halas
17. 118
18. 15,710
19. 13
20. Three
21. 1953, 1954 and 1957
22. Two (1954 and 1956)
23. Green Bay (The final score was 13-13.)
24. Quarterbacks coach (1963-1965)
25. Dallas Cowboys
26. 243
27. 1956
28. 1968 (November 17)
29. *Heart of a Lion:The Wild and Wooly Life of Bobby Layne*
30. Doak Walker

3 - Joe Schmidt
1. Paul
2. Brentwood High School in Pennsylvania
3. Fullback
4. Pittsburgh Steelers
5. Seventh
6. Eight
7. 154
8. 1960
9. Nine
10. 10 (1955-1964)
11. Four (1955, '57, '58, '61)
12. 24
13. Three
14. 43
15. 34 (One tie also)

4 - Barry Sanders
1. North High School
2. The Lions Media Guide lists him at 5' 9". (He is generally listed as 5' 8".)
3. Oklahoma
4. Thurman Thomas
5. Marcus Allen
6. 7.6 yards
7. Byron "Whizzer" White
8. Rodney Peete
9. Five
10. $6.1 million
11. 18 yards
12. 71 (on nine carries)
13. Chicago Bears (He rushed for 126 yards in the game.)
14. Five
15. 118 (23.6 yard average)
16. 1,470
17. 14
18. Bob Gagliano (22 yards)
19. 1,304
20. He became the first non-kicker in club history to score over 100 points (102) in a single season.
21. Cincinnati Bengals
22. November 22, 1992
23. Houston Oilers (It was incomplete.)
24. 1,115
25. 169 (27 attempts)
26. 237
27. Tampa Bay—November 13, 1994

28. 40
29. 194
30. 85 yards vs. Tampa Bay on October 2, 1994 (He lost his shoe during the run.)
31. The play set a record for the longest run ever at the Silverdome.
32. Three (against Dallas on September 19; against Tampa Bay on November 13; against Minnesota on December 17)
33. NFL Performer of the Year
34. "The Late Show With David Letterman"
35. Green Bay in Milwaukee (December 6, 1992)

GENERAL FACTS & TRIVIA

1 - The Hall of Fame
1. Hugh McElhenny, Ollie Matson and Frank Gatski
2. McElhenny ('64), Matson ('63) and Gatski ('57)
3. 35
4. 50
5. Five
6. Four
7. Buddy Morrow
8. 14
9. 81
10. Charlie "Choo Choo" Justice
11. Robert
12. Four
13. Texas A & M
14. 1959, 1961 and 1963
15. Nine
16. Ewell Doak Walker II
17. Five
18. "Mumbles"
19. Doak Walker
20. Jackson State
21. Seven
22. Philadelphia Eagles (He still had a year of college eligibility. One year later, the Lions drafted him.)
23. 76
24. William & Mary
25. Doak Walker

2 - Coaches' Corner
1. Gus Dorais
2. Nugent
3. Philadelphia Eagles
4. Two (He resigned before the third game after being diagnosed with cancer.)
5. Klein
6. San Francisco 49ers (Detroit won the game by a score of 24-7.)
7. Los Angeles Rams (Lions won, 34-17.)
8. Tampa Bay Buccaneers
9. Potsy Clark, Buddy Parker and George Wilson
10. Dutch Clark, Buddy Parker, Harry Gilmer and Joe Schmidt

3 - Grab Bag
1. Honolulu blue and silver
2. Chicago Bears
3. Cleveland Browns
4. Cleveland Browns
5. Wayne Walker
6. "Gridiron Heroes—The Victory Song of the Detroit Lions"
7. Graham T. Overgard
8. 1935-1936
9. Four (1935, 1952, 1953 and 1957)
10 LA Rams (65 points on October 29, 1950)
11. *Paper Lion*
12. George Plimpton
13. *Sports Illustrated*
14. Alan Alda
15. Arizona Cardinals (They were the Chicago Cardinals when Portsmouth first played them in 1930.)
16. Two (Danielson and Mitchell)
17. Bobby Layne (118 yards on September 24, 1950 vs. Pittsburgh)
18. Two
19. Bobby Layne and Greg Landry
20. Eight
21. Bob Hoernschemeyer, Doak Walker, Pat Harder, Nick Pietrosante, Mel Farr, Steve Owens, Billy Sims and Barry Sanders.
22. Dutch Clark, Doak Walker, Cloyce Box and

Barry Sanders
23. 19
24. Eight
25. Frank Sinkwich, Doak Walker, Leon Hart, Howard Cassady, Steve Owens, Billy Sims, Barry Sanders and Andre Ware (Gino Torretta was on the Lions' roster in '94, but he never played.)
26. Bobby Layne
27. Lem Barney, Billy Sims and Barry Sanders
28. Mike Lucci
29. Edsel Ford
30. William Clay Ford, Jr.
31. 15 (seven wins, eight losses)
32. 1) actor: Tim Allen; 2) show: Home Improvement
33. Six
34. Dutch Clark, Bobby Layne, Doak Walker, Joe Schmidt, Chuck Hughes and Charlie Sanders
35. Three (Frank Sinkwich, Leon Hart and Billy Sims)

About the Author

Marc Davis was born in Conneaut, Pennsylvania, but he grew up in Oshkosh, Wisconsin, where he lives today. In between, he has lived for brief periods in Kingsville, Ohio; Nashua, New Hampshire; Lawrence, Massachusetts; Rockland, Maine; and Oklahoma City, Oklahoma. *Detroit Lions Facts & Trivia* is his first book.

His personal interests include collecting books and movies—classics as well as current releases—and he is an avid sports fan.

Davis admits its not easy being a Lions fan in Packerland, but he says: "Some of my best friends are Packer fans, so it's hard to hold a grudge against them. The rivalry is all in good fun."

Davis and his twin brother share a residence with their two dogs, Vixie and Noah. Marc works as assistant manager for a major grocery store, and he works part-time at his father's flying school in Oshkosh.